"There is always the temptation to create a counterfeit version of Jesus born out of our imaginations. The sad reality is that Jesus is too often flattened into a one-dimensional figure and co-opted for someone's agenda. In this refreshing and insightful book, we are confronted with who Jesus actually was, the real deal according to Scripture. This Jesus wants to remake us in his image—and not the other way around. Read this wonderful book with your Bible open and your heart as well."

—Nijay K. Gupta, Julius R. Mantey Professor of New Testament, Northern Seminary

"In a time when the only Jesus that people generally see is in the political sphere, *Jesus Was* offers a refreshing and much-needed perspective. Through thirty-one engaging essays, the book reintroduces readers to the transformative and deeply human Jesus of the Gospels, challenging assumptions and offering insights. With contributions from a diverse group of theologians and ministers, this collection not only explores who Jesus was but also inspires readers to see how his life and teachings remain profoundly relevant in today's world. This is a book that brings Jesus out of the headlines and back into our hearts."

—Pastor Josh Burtram and Will Wright, hosts of the podcast *Faithful Politics*

"The title and subtitle say it all. *Jesus Was: Not What We Expected but Better Than We Imagined* is a collection of insightful essays that brim with everyday stories, humorous asides, and humble observations. Biblically sound and theologically astute, the authors reflect on Jesus's life with such creativity and honesty that Jesus becomes real and personal in concrete and beautiful ways. The authors share personal stories but are never preachy. They tackle life's tough realities with compassion, challenging established norms and inviting reflection. The reader comes away trusting more deeply in the Jesus who is all we hope for and more."

—Lynn H. Cohick, Distinguished Professor of New Testament, Houston Christian University

"We are often encouraged to 'be Jesus with skin on,' meaning, treat others like Jesus would. In *Jesus Was*, we discover the Jesus who had skin and flesh and emotions as he traveled the roads of Israel. The authors invite us to walk alongside the embodied Son of God as he loved with all his heart, mind, and body, and to love our neighbors the way Jesus loved his. The essays within reflect on the remarkably relatable humanity of our still very divine Savior."

—Kelley Mathews, coauthor of *40 Questions About Women in Ministry*

"*Jesus Was* is a fresh wind for today. Filled with new, necessary voices and keen spiritual insights, this book invites the reader to get to know Jesus—again or for the first time—through clear lenses of theological acumen, profundity, delight, and above all, worship."

—Aubrey Sampson, church planter, podcaster, and author of *What We Find in the Dark* and *The Louder Song*

"We have a tendency to slap the word *Christian* on almost anything—books, podcasts, churches, stores, ideologies—and assume that the label means Christ followers will find Jesus there. But do we know who Jesus was, what he looked like, how he behaved, what he valued? Jesus was a historical person with a notable way of being in the world—a kingdom way that defies American marketing efforts. I invite you to sit down with this collection of essays and immerse yourself in who Jesus was. Bring your whole heart and mind, and find God in these pages."

—Catherine McNiel, author of *Fearing Bravely*

"In a world where groups often portray Jesus in ways that advance their religious, political, or moral agendas, *Jesus Was* offers a refreshing return to who he actually was. If you've been discouraged by trends in today's church, this compelling collection will reconnect you with the authentic Jesus—reminding you that who he was then is exactly who he is now."

—Kathi Lipp, author of *Sabbath Soup*

FOREWORD BY SCOT MCKNIGHT

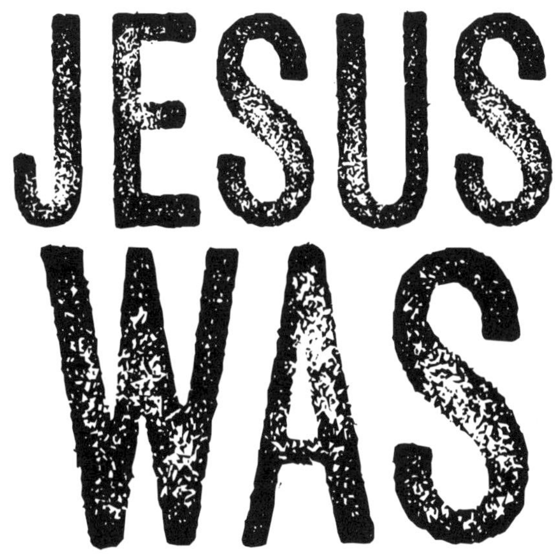

not what we
expected but
better than we
imagined

SUSY FLORY &
SCOTT JOHANNINGSMEIER
EDITORS

Jesus Was: Not What We Expected but Better Than We Imagined

Published by Kregel Publications, a division of Kregel Inc., 2450 Oak Industrial Dr. NE, Grand Rapids, MI 49505. www.kregel.com.

Published in association with Gardner Literary, LLC. www.gardner-literary.com.

The persons and events portrayed in this book have been used with permission. To protect the privacy of these individuals, some names and identifying details have been changed.

Italics in Scripture quotations indicate the authors' added emphasis.

Cataloging-in-Publication Data is available from the Library of Congress.

ISBN 978-0-8254-4956-7, print
ISBN 978-0-8254-4958-1, epub
ISBN 978-0-8254-4957-4, Kindle

Printed in the United States of America
25 26 27 28 29 30 31 32 33 34 / 5 4 3 2 1

This book is for those who love Jesus
and want to be reminded of the Jesus of the Gospels,
those who are willing to step outside of assumptions
and comfort zones to rediscover the Jesus of the Gospels,
and those who are willing to push their own boundaries
and investigate what is beautiful about Jesus.

Contents

Foreword

One of the most dramatic moments in the Gospels, at the literary level, is an incident reported in Mark 4:35–41. In this episode Jesus embarks with his apprentices to the other side of the Sea of Galilee to escape the growing crowd. The crowd made Herod Antipas nervous as he lived in Tiberias, an easy distance from Capernaum, where Jesus was. During their trip across the lake, a fierce storm erupts. The apprentices perceive they are on the threshold of death while Jesus is sound asleep in the stern of the boat. It's an easy scene to imagine because the author is using an ancient technique called *ekphrasis*, that is, the purposeful use of vivid language to stimulate the emotions and persuade readers or listeners to embrace Jesus. After the apprentices express dismay with Jesus, the Lord silences the storm. But the most dramatic moment of this vivid scene is the one that brings down the curtain on the paragraph. The apprentices in the boat ask, "Who is this? Even the wind and the waves obey him!" (Mark 4:41). "Who is Jesus?" is the ultimate question of evangelism. The answer to that question reveals the condition of the one being asked.

When I heard from the editors of this volume that students, now my friends, were responding affirmatively to writing essays with the opening title "Jesus Was . . . ," I was excited as one of their professors—a professor who tries to motivate students to write—and even more so as one who believes the question and answers at work in this book are fundamental to the health of the church.

Too many churches, pastors, and ministry leaders think first about salvation and church growth and status and spiritual gifts but not enough about Jesus—who he was, what he did, and what he said, thus the need for answers to such questions. I am so proud of these essays. Whether one would like other answers to other questions or not, or even if one would affirm what these students affirm differently, the right conversation has been opened. In this book you will be wondering who Jesus was and is. No subject is more important.

The question "Who is Jesus?" is asked often in the Gospels. Here's a list of some of the occurrences:

> The Pharisees and the teachers of the law began thinking to themselves, "*Who is this* fellow who speaks blasphemy? Who can forgive sins but God alone?" (Luke 5:21)
>
> The other guests began to say among themselves, "*Who is this* who even forgives sins?" (7:49)
>
> But Herod said, "I beheaded John. *Who, then, is this* I hear such things about?" And he tried to see him. (9:9)
>
> When Jesus entered Jerusalem, the whole city was stirred and asked, "*Who is this*?" (Matthew 21:10)
>
> The crowd spoke up, "We have heard from the Law that the Messiah will remain forever, so how can you say, 'The Son of Man must be lifted up'? *Who is this* 'Son of Man'?" (John 12:34)

Pharisees and theological experts asked this question. Guests who saw Jesus pronounce forgiveness also asked this question. Herod Antipas asked it too. With more than a little touch of hyperbole, Matthew informs us that the whole city of Jerusalem was asking it. And an entire crowd in the gospel of John asked it as well.

What the various groups implied in asking this question was just as diverse: Who but a blasphemer thinks he can *forgive sins*? Who could have the powers to heal people and exorcise unclean spirits, except for John the Baptist come back to life? After all, John had been decapitated for speaking against Herod's marriage to Herodias (see Mark 6:14–29). The powers at work in Jesus must be explained as the powers at work in John. Who in the world would enter the city of Jerusalem on a donkey, mocking Rome's generals who enter with pomp and power displays? Who would enter the city with such a ragtag bunch of Judeans and Galileans, acting like the king of Israel? Like the Messiah? Who speaks of the Son of Man from Daniel 7 as if he was the one who would ascend before the Ancient of Days?

Jesus stirred people to ask who in the world he could be. When he spoke up in his hometown synagogue in Nazareth, the people asked three questions: "Where did this man get these things? . . . What's this wisdom that has been given him? What are these remarkable miracles he is performing?" Those questions were chased down with a query similar to the question, "Who is Jesus?" The locals asked, "Isn't this the carpenter? Isn't this Mary's son and the brother of James, Joseph, Judas and Simon? Aren't his sisters here with us?" (Mark 6:2–3). They tripped over who Jesus *was*, not what he had done or what he said. They "took offense at *him*."

The best readings of the Gospels concentrate our attention on the central subject and the premier actor of each paragraph—Jesus. Not a theology, not a creed, not a philosophy, not a theory. A person. When I translated the New Testament for *The Second Testament* and was given the privilege of labeling each paragraph, I did all I could to make *Jesus* the first word in each header. Every passage of the New Testament is about Jesus, not us. We may learn discipleship in these passages, but when we wrongly turn them into messages *about* us instead of *for* us, we misread the Gospels along with the rest of the books in the New Testament. Each passage truly is about Jesus: Messiah, Lord, Lamb of God, Son of Man, Son of God, Savior, coming King, and the Lion of Judah. The best readings of the New Testament ponder Jesus so thoroughly that we lift our heads, close our eyes, and see Jesus—who he is, what he did, and what he is asking of us. It's a skill we may need to learn, but one thing I can tell you: *Jesus Was* will help you become a skilled reader of the Bible who sees Jesus as the message of the Bible.

Scot McKnight
Visiting Professor at Houston Theological Seminary and
Westminster Theological Centre

The Story of *Jesus Was*

SUSY FLORY

I was standing in the Haitian sun, sweating in rumpled clothes, when I saw Jesus.

I was there to research a book project about a young woman who bought six acres of land and built a school for five hundred children in an impoverished area. Even today, Haiti has still not yet recovered from the devastating 2010 earthquake. The country is currently embroiled in acute political and civil unrest and is considered the poorest country in the Western Hemisphere. A doctor who has done much humanitarian work in Haiti once said that while many Haitians are in poverty, all the people in Haiti are in *misery*.

The enthusiasm and faith woven into this beautiful work of God had drawn others who wanted to help, like Nolan. A competitive soccer player with a dark curly mop of hair and a huge white-toothed smile, he came to Haiti to run sports programs for the school. Nolan was kind of a goofball, always breaking into a song or a dance and laughing or playing with the kids. You could tell Haiti had captured his heart.

One humid, sunny afternoon I was at the school, standing and looking out over the edge of the property at the sparkling blue Caribbean Sea. Then I turned back and looked deep into the towering mountains covered by a tangle of mysterious jungle, dotted with tiny shacks and rising curls of smoke from cooking fires. A movement caught my eye. I looked back and it was Nolan, standing about fifty feet away on the grass between the school buildings. It was recess, and three or four of the first graders were mobbing him, jumping on his back and trying to climb up his legs. I watched as he stood still, looking down at the children as they laughed and chattered in Creole and clamored for his attention. Just then he must've felt my gaze and he looked up straight at me, and he smiled the biggest smile I've ever seen. It was like a physical jolt—the pure happiness of the kids and the intense joy on Nolan's face. It wrecked me.

In that small moment, he was Jesus to me. I can't explain it; I just know it. And now I know there is hope. The problems in Haiti are overwhelming, but there are places where Jesus walks and plays with his children. And I know because I saw him.

Have you ever wondered what Jesus was like? I mean, really like? Was he serious or casual? Was he street smart or formally educated? Was he politically minded or influential? What was his personality like? What was his character like? What was he like as a *person*? One way to begin to get to know him better is by taking a fresh look at Jesus through what he said and did while he was on the earth. Centuries of church teachings and scholarly investigation sometimes complicate the simplicity of the stories of Jesus from the Gospels and take away from the actual stories of those who knew him best—his friends, followers, and family.

Jesus isn't a stained-glass window or just some character in a story—he was a real person who lived and breathed, ate and slept, worked and played, laughed and cried. But everywhere he went, he changed people, culture, and history. He had friends, disciples, students, and followers of all kinds, but he lived a long time ago, and sometimes what he said and did can seem distant. Jesus can feel more like a concept, belief, or dry historical fact than an actual person.

But Jesus was a real person, and this is a book about getting to know him better by looking at his life on earth. This book was born in an unusual way. Feeling unmoored by the chaotic and frightening events unfolding at the US Capitol on January 6, I wanted to do something, so I posted three simple words on a popular social media outlet: "Jesus was nonviolent."[1] Those three words drew many comments, most of them thoughtful and affirming. The next day, I posted another "Jesus was" statement. More comments appeared. And I kept going.

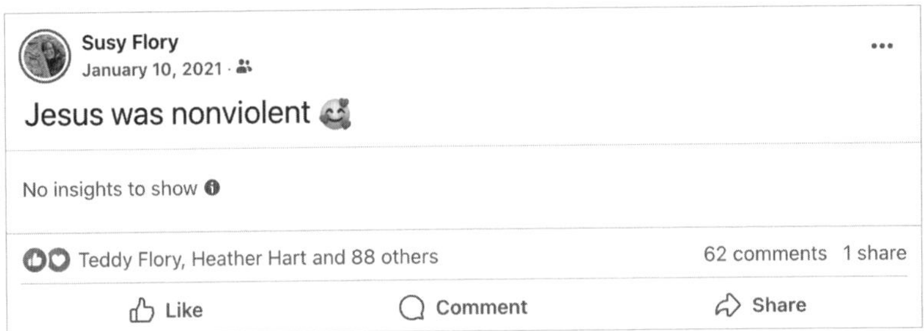

Each day for thirty days, I posted three to five words about the character and behavior of Jesus, and it opened some amazing conversations in the midst of an onslaught of rhetoric, anger, frustration, and fear coming from all directions. I expected people to argue more, but I think there was something about looking at Jesus's words and actions that calmed us and gave us hope and an anchor when the country seemed to be reeling. People in the "Jesus was" conversation shared thoughts of all kinds in terms of politics, faith, and religion (or no religion at all). The conversation was remarkably civil, and many observers were curious, wanting to remember or discover for the first time who Jesus actually was.

Invariably on almost every post someone would remark, "Jesus *is*" to my "Jesus *was*" statement. Sometimes I let it go, but other times I gently explained this was about what Jesus said and did with skin on, when he was here on earth.

Jesus Was is a collection of short pieces inspired by that unexpected, monthlong conversation. These chapters were written by a group of diverse, smart, hardworking, passionate, and caring people I've been going to seminary with, people who love Jesus and who have dedicated their lives to helping others get to know him too. These short chapters and the discovery questions that follow are meant to be read through, discussed, and savored.

The thoughtful essays were written by theologically minded ministers who have boots on the ground and a heart wide open for a hurting, polarized church amid a culture of deconstruction and collective trauma. We want to reclaim Jesus, one "Jesus was" at a time, and let him be who he truly was: God in a human body, showing us what God is like and doing what he was sent to do—reclaim us as his precious brothers and sisters.

The reality is we often shape Jesus into our own image. We read the Gospels through our own filters and often practice a form of Christianity of our own design. This is not a new development. Throughout history people have molded Christianity to fit their desires and passions. In response, there has always been a call back to the biblical text. *Jesus Was* is our response, by examining different characteristics of Jesus as revealed in the Bible.

It's time to let go of the old, stale, and sometimes even scary images of Jesus that may be hanging around your heart and soul, and to try something different. In *Jesus Was*, we hope you will meet Jesus in a whole new way through some of the fresh new voices in the church. If you've ever wondered who Jesus *really* was, you're in for a restart.

In this book, we are raising our voices together in an effort to wash away all the unexamined dogma, inherited misconceptions, and inaccurate depictions that have built up in layers over the years, and instead create a beautiful and vibrant kaleidoscope of who Jesus truly was.

Chapter 1

Jesus Was a Listener

ELIZABETH DAIGLE

Therefore consider carefully how you listen.
—LUKE 8:18

My friend is a jazz musician. I love to watch him up on stage because he plays his guitar with his whole body, not just his hands. His eyes are closed, his brow is furrowed, and his head is cocked ever so slightly to enhance his concentration. He sways with the swells of the melody. His legs keep step. Even his breathing matches the cadence. He chooses a thread from the melody and weaves each musical element together so seamlessly that it feels as if what is being played has always been a part of the composition. But unlike weavers, who use their eyes to create a tapestry with a collection of colored strands, my friend uses his ears. Improvisation is amazing, almost deceiving. Because the ability to take a few notes and morph them into the start of a whole new movement doesn't come easily. It begins with musical gifting and years of study but to truly master improvisation requires a practiced discipline of listening.

I'd like to think if Jesus were a musician, he'd play jazz. There's something about the spontaneity of jazz music that seems to fit him well. I imagine Jesus would be the master of retooling a melody. He would make the simplest one soar. He'd send it singing with a twist so winsome and surprising that anyone within earshot would be awestruck. That is, if they were listening. Real listening is *hard*. We hear lots of things, but we listen selectively. And while it is a wise and self-protective strategy on some levels, in our attempts to block out all the noise, we also sometimes block out the voices we need to hear in the process.

Noise is my constant companion here in the city. When I open my front door, I'm greeted by the hum of a city that never settles. A bus accelerating up the hill, a helicopter descending upon the hospital-roof landing pad, the whirl of sirens and horns. And while Jesus didn't deal with the din of machinery and all manner of electronics, he did endure the constant pursuit of people. Like many of us, Jesus was surrounded by noise.

Escaping the Noise and Learning to Listen

As word about Jesus spread, so did the intensity of the crowds pressing in on him. To combat the clamor, the Gospels tell us, Jesus walked away, not from the people but from the noise. He applied himself to the discipline of solitude because he understood that *ministering well* begins with *listening well.*

Jesus withdrew to lonely, secluded places to pray. He retreated to the mountains by himself (Mark 1:35; 6:46; Luke 6:12). He left for the wilderness not to abandon the desperate but to abandon himself to the singular voice of the Father. He didn't leave the crowds because of their demands or the enormity of their needs but because he understood that the only way to minister to them was to begin with listening. He needed to hear from the Father so he could hear the cries of the people.

I imagine Jesus's discipline of listening, forged in the secret place of communion with the Father, was woven together with his ability to discern. He respectfully refused to multitask and instead was fully present with whoever stood before him. As a keen observer, Jesus offered his full attention and listened not just with his ears but also with his eyes, touch, and every sensitivity of his soul. And as a result, he heard more than the words and requests of those who approached him. He heard the hidden cries of their hearts.

Answering a question with a question was a common teaching technique of Jesus (e.g., Matthew 15:1–3; Mark 2:1–11; 4:38–40). His intent wasn't to be evasive or coy but to allow the questioner the privilege of self-discovery. Jesus used this technique to tease out motives and probe at agendas but also to introduce deeper truths to his audiences, providing all who heard with an opportunity to learn.

Jesus respectfully refused to multitask and instead was fully present with whoever stood before him.

Jesus used this approach to tee up teachable moments that often served as preambles to his parables. Luke recorded such an exchange between Jesus and an expert in the religious law (Luke 10:25–29). The man begins by asking Jesus how he might inherit eternal life. "What is written in the Law?" Jesus asks him in reply. "How do you read it?" The man answers by reciting the Old Testament law: "You must love the Lord your God with all your heart, all your soul, all your strength, and all your mind, and love your neighbor as yourself." Jesus affirms his correct recitation, declaring, "Do this and you will live!" But in verse 29, Jesus's answer really wasn't what the man was after, so he then asks Jesus his real question, "And who is my neighbor?" Hearing and understanding what the man was truly asking, Jesus does more than simply answer his question. He challenges the man's attempt to justify himself and put people into the neat and tidy categories of those who are worthy of being called neighbors and those who are not. Jesus listens with discernment and stuns the man by upending his preexisting view of righteousness through the story of the Good Samaritan (Luke 10:30–37).

This kind of exchange between Jesus and the religious authorities of his day is repeated over and over. On one occasion Jesus was accused of associating—even eating!—with sinful people like tax collectors. The religious elite were particularly offended because those who collected taxes from the Jews to hand over to Rome were considered traitors. How could Jesus suffer through a meal with the likes of them? But once again, Jesus rejects their labels and hears their hearts. He goes on to share a trio of parables about lost things (Luke 15). And I wonder, as these elites listened to Jesus describe the shepherd's pursuit of the lost sheep, the woman searching for the lost coin, and the father awaiting the return of his lost son, if they had ears to hear the truth about who really was lost after all.

Listening to Those Without a Voice

The children certainly seemed to have ears to hear Jesus. Maybe it's because he opened his arms and listened to them. The gospel of Luke describes a scene in which parents bring their little children to Jesus for a blessing (Luke 18:15–17). The disciples are aghast, scolding the parents for bothering the master. But Jesus, always unhurried, takes the time to gather these little ones up in his arms. He honors them with his time and offers them his complete attention. You can almost picture the tenderness of the scene as Jesus gazes into their eyes with kindness and interest, asking them questions about themselves and waiting patiently for their answers. The disciples saw the kids as irritating intrusions. Jesus saw them as precious gifts and announced that the kingdom of God belonged to them.

There were many more like the children who were invisible to the broader Roman society but were nevertheless visible to Jesus. Luke's gospel records what happened when a blind beggar realizes Jesus was part of a crowd about to pass by him on the road to Jericho (Luke 18:35–42). The blind man shouts, "Jesus, Son of David, have mercy on me!" The crowd yells at him to stop, but he only shouts louder. When Jesus finally hears him call, he goes over to the blind man. But rather than immediately restore his sight, Jesus asks him what he wants and then listens for his reply. When the man says, "I want to see," Jesus responds with mercy and healing. Jesus heard his cry for help, listened to his plea, and then moved in compassion to heal. Jesus hasn't changed. He still hears our cries, and he still moves in compassion.

When Jesus's mission on earth was complete, he ascended to the Father and now sits in a place of honor in heaven. In the book of Romans we're told Jesus pleads for us from his place at the Father's right hand (Romans 8:34). You see, Jesus has never stopped listening. He listened during his years on earth, and he continues to listen from heaven. But like the beggar by the side of the road, we must do our part and call. And we must call out to him in faith, even faith as small as a mustard seed.

I want to learn how to listen with everything I've got, like my friend the jazz musician. I want to be so connected and feel the nuance of the melody so powerfully that I sway, losing myself in the music. To do that, I need to take my cues not from the others in the band, but from the one who conducts heaven and earth. I need to strive to listen for Jesus in the same way he listened for his Father. Then I must use what I hear to tune my ear to the people around me and practice listening, just like Jesus.

---

1. Is there a physical place you find calming? What aspects of that location feels restorative to you?
2. Is there someone in your life who is good at being fully present when they are with you? What do they do to show they are not distracted when they're with you? How does their bodily presence affect you?
3. What barriers in your community keep some members from feeling seen or heard? Are there ways for you to intentionally see and hear people on the periphery in a personal way?

Explore: Listen to a favorite song. Write out why you like it and how it affects your body and emotions.

Chapter 2

Jesus Was Nonviolent

CODY MATCHETT

> *"Put your sword back in its place," Jesus said to him, "for all who draw the sword will die by the sword."*
>
> —Matthew 26:52

Have you ever experienced violence? My hope is you have not experienced physical violence in a personal way, although some of you reading this probably have. But even if you have not experienced an assault yourself, you have likely witnessed one, whether in real life, in a movie or television show, or in a video game. But violence can take other forms, such as verbal or emotional assaults, which you likely have experienced in some form. It's impossible to live among other human beings and not be exposed to violence; it is part of the human condition and why many of us who bear, or care for, children would love to surround them in bubble wrap at times and keep them safe from violence in any form.

In his poem *Heroides*, the Roman writer Ovid penned the infamous words *exitus acta probat*, "the outcome justifies the deeds" (2.85). These words have been reconceptualized and disseminated in many ways since then, perhaps most famously in our saying "the ends justify the means." At its core, the phrase suggests that *wrong actions* may be necessary to achieve *desired outcomes*. The phrase highlights that, as human beings within a complex world, we may modify our own standards of morality to achieve certain results: *deception* to preserve self-perception, *cheating* to get ahead, *cutting corners* on projects to serve the bottom line, *misusing our power* to circumvent political processes to benefit certain groups, or *exacting violence* to secure "safety" and "freedom." In other words, we justify morally objectionable activities to secure or maintain our desired outcomes. In surveying history, it is clear that human beings are willing participants in many morally objectionable activities to achieve their goals, but one activity in particular stands out among the rest: *violence*. Humans will enact violence against others to achieve security, freedom, and peace.

Jesus Refused Violent Means

The use of violence as a tool to achieve certain goals was the way of the Roman Empire. The phrase "peace of Rome" (*Pax Romana*) was an axiom of central importance to the ideology and propaganda by which the Roman emperors and the elites that served them legitimated their rule. For example, the emperor Augustus, who showcased peace through violence and force, erected inscriptions across the empire that celebrated him as the one "who has made war to cease and who will put everything in . . . order" (Priene Inscription, lines 36–37). The first-century BC poet Virgil lauded Rome as "making peace the way of life for humanity" (*Aeneid* 6.851–53), and coins were frequently minted by Roman emperors, such as Tiberius and Vespasian, during this period depicting Pax, the deified personification of peace.[1] Yet even when celebrating peace, Rome acknowledged the role of military violence in securing peace. The Altar of Peace, completed in 9 BC to celebrate Caesar Augustus, displayed Pax on one side along with the goddess Roma, symbol of Rome, embodying the military power of the Roman Empire. Pairing these two figures together, Pax and Roma, reveals the truth about the empire, which was really pacification and compliance enforced by threat of arms. Caesar's peace depended on violence.[2]

Rome was not the first to use corporal punishments such as beheadings or even crucifixion, but they perfected these cruel practices. One such instance of the violent brutality of the Roman Empire was when Crassus crucified more than six thousand slaves. The crucifixions were visible along the roads from Capua to Rome as a warning and deterrent against stepping out of line. Rome was not satisfied by simply ending the lives of those who the state considered the worst of the worst. No, Rome chose to brutalize and obliterate all honor and dignity in order to force conformity.[3] All of that to say, the Roman Empire, along with every other empire that has existed on this earth, was willing to use violence to achieve their ends.

However, according to Jesus of Nazareth, such ends will never be achieved by corrupted means. In stark contrast to the kingdoms of this world, the means of Jesus were nonviolent. In the Sermon on the Mount, Jesus offers his manifesto for life in the kingdom of God, including these groundbreaking words about life in his kingdom:

> But I tell you, do not resist an evil person. If anyone slaps you on the right cheek, turn to them the other cheek also. And if anyone wants to sue you and take your shirt, hand over your coat as well. If anyone forces you to go one mile, go with them two miles. Give to the one who asks you, and do not turn away from the one who wants to borrow from you. (Matthew 5:39–42)

These scenarios presented by Jesus are not hypothetical situations, but rather they come from real experiences of people under the subjugation of the Roman Empire: being insulted and physically mistreated, being sued in court, being conscripted to support the Roman military, and being forced to give up resources to another. According to Jesus, the only way to resist the downward cycle of violence is by refusing to mirror the violent injustices of the world, because violence only begets more violence. It must never be used to resist evil but instead must be borne and suffered (Romans 12:21; 1 Peter 5:6–11).

Jesus embodied nonviolence not only in his life and teaching (Matthew 5:3–9; Mark 14:43–52; 15:16–20; Luke 6:27–38) but also most importantly in his death on the Roman cross—bearing the weight of violence, alienation, and shame, extending forgiveness, and welcoming his enemies into the garden of God (Luke 23:34). While violence destroys and disintegrates, loving our enemies and praying for our persecutors leads to our becoming whole, just as our Father is whole (Matthew 5:48). We must refuse the means of the world's oppressive structures, because without the *means* of Jesus we will never experience the *ends* of Jesus, the kingdom of God.

While violence destroys and disintegrates, loving our enemies and praying for our persecutors leads to our becoming whole.

Instead of harnessing violence as a means to an end, Jesus urges his apprentices to resist evil by means of active nonviolence by putting away our weapons (Matthew 26:52) and through doing good to our "enemies" (Luke 6:35). Rather than retaliating with violence, followers of Jesus are to stand firm, to speak truth to corrupted powers, to "insist on our common humanity, disarm our opponent, risk suffering love, trust in God, and work for the conversion of our opponent, so that the one who does evil or supports systemic injustice, changes."[4] Jesus's response when a large crowd with swords and clubs approached to arrest him was to speak to them. "Am I leading a rebellion, that you have come out with swords and clubs to capture me? Every day I sat in the temple courts teaching, and you did not arrest me" (Matthew 26:55).

Jesus calls us to seek the transformation of our enemies into our kin and the renovation of their hearts, so that they might be won into the kingdom of peace. The early church took this message to heart, and when a crowd stoned Stephen, he prayed, "Lord, do not hold this sin against them" (Acts 7:60). A young man named Saul was a part of the crowd, and he went out breathing murderous threats against the followers of Jesus. While Stephen died before seeing the result of his prayer, Saul met the resurrected Christ on the road to Damascus and became a follower of Jesus (Acts 9). We know him as Paul, the author of many of the New Testament letters.

Nonviolence, however, should not be replaced with passivity but with active nonviolent resistance. In other words, Jesus does not urge passive resignation or indifference to all the violent evil of the world, but instead models steadfast resistance to violence and injustice by loving enemies and praying for persecutors (Matthew 5:43–44). Jesus urges us to follow him, which means to embody *self-sacrificial, cruciform love* that conforms to the narrative and patterns of Jesus as the standard for a life.[5] Following Jesus, then, means to bear evil, deconstruct it, and render it powerless so that the kingdom of God might come on earth as it is in heaven.[6]

Following the Means of Jesus

As a pastor and teacher, I have noticed two common responses to Jesus's teachings on nonviolence. The first is the creation of *exceptive clauses* to justify the necessity of violent activities (e.g., just-war theory). In this category, people seem to know that Jesus taught nonviolence, but they rationalize the necessary exceptions that must be made to secure nation and freedom. The second response is *undercutting* the clear teachings of Jesus by prioritizing or misreading other sections of the Scriptures. In this category, people point to conquest narratives or instances of Jesus with a whip in the temple or a sword in final judgment. But they fail to realize that the conquest is not normative, the whip is solely used on animals (John 2:15), and the sword is coming out of his mouth, which symbolizes his spoken word (Revelation 19:11–16; cf. Hebrews 4:12–13).

So, if while we were enemies of God Jesus died for us, how are we to act toward our enemies (Romans 5:7–9)? While they are still our enemies, we must die for them. We must lay ourselves down, surrendering for the sake of others. We must allow life-giving love to turn our enemy into our neighbor, and manifest life patterned after the ways of Jesus. In the kingdom of God, we have no right to deny someone love when Jesus has lovingly died on their behalf. As noted by N. T. Wright, we are called—as the reconciled humanity, the people of God in the world—to become "a place of reconciliation between God and the world; a place where humans might be reconciled to one another; a *microcosmos* in which the world is contained in a nutshell as a sign of what God intends to do for the whole creation; a new sort of polis in which heaven and earth come together."[7]

The nonviolent way of Jesus might mean *responding to insult with kindness* rather than retaliation; *loving and praying for those who mistreat you* rather than seeking revenge; *engaging in civil disobedience to confront injustice* rather than using violent means; *performing acts of service with compassion toward your perceived enemies* rather than seeking their harm; *advocating for restorative justice* rather than destructive retribution; and *choosing to turn the other cheek* rather than exacting righteous indignation. There is no simple prescription for embodying the nonviolent way of Jesus. We live in a complex, confusing, and chaotic world, but for followers of Jesus, one thing is clear: The ends will never be achieved by corrupted means.

The *means* of Jesus were nonviolent.

Jesus taught that the only way to counter evil is not with more evil but rather with suffering in the form of self-sacrificial, cross-shaped love for our enemies because "evil will [only] become powerless when it finds no opposing object, no resistance, but, instead, is willingly borne and suffered. Evil [then] meets an opponent for which it is not a match."[8] In following the nonviolent way of Jesus, we may not be able to stop all the violence, but we can be a prophetic witness as we saw in Stephen. We can shine the light of Jesus in our world's darkest hours. We might not be able to avoid being affected by all forms of violence, though we might try. Instead, we must hold each other steady, knowing we are not alone. Together we can make a stand against the violence of this world as followers of the one who taught us to "love your enemies and pray for those who persecute you" (Matthew 5:44).

---

1. How do you define *violence*? How is violence always related to bodily harm? Have you seen or experienced violence as a justification for achieving security, freedom, or peace?
2. Who do you know that models active nonviolence? How does your community respond to those who offer alternatives to violence?
3. Think of vulnerable people groups in your community. How do they experience violence? What might active nonviolence look like on their behalf?

Explore: Read a book by a Christian who advocates for active nonviolence, such as Martin Luther King Jr.'s *Stride Toward Freedom: The Montgomery Story*. Reflect on how your body and emotions respond to these ideas.

Chapter 3

Jesus Was New

SUSY FLORY

Jesus is the Gospel.[1]
—Scot McKnight

Not long ago I finished a project for work, and after hundreds of hours of staring at my computer screen, I decided to do something different and work with my hands. I brought home two small metal cans from the hardware store and spent the next week brushing thick creamy white paint over my old golden oak kitchen cabinets—what a transformation from dark and dingy to bright, white, and new. I can't get over how different the cabinets look, and how my eyes keep picking out new details. I can't stop staring.

When something is new, it's beautiful, fresh, and clean, leaving what is old behind and offering promise and hope for the future. In many ways Jesus was new. To start with, never before had God put on a human body—a brand new human baby's skin and frame at that—to live among humanity on the earth he had created. This was completely new. It had never happened before, and we're still not quite sure exactly how it worked. But it did, and God took on flesh. God as a human baby? What a novel idea!

Strange and unusual events surrounded his birth. An angel named Gabriel, who stood in the presence of God, visited his mother to let her know what was about to happen (Luke 1:26–28). This was news to Mary, who had never been with a man. Yet, faced with this very unexpected situation, she responded with great faith and accepted the message and her mission—to birth, nurture, and raise the Son of God. When Jesus was born, odd visitors came to see him, including local shepherds summoned by heralding angels and wise men summoned by a star. This was followed by a flight to Egypt to escape death at the hands of a bloodthirsty ruler.

After that, his life went quiet for a couple of decades with nothing much to report. Jesus went about his business, making things with his hands, going to synagogue with his family, and being part of his village, and it wasn't until he was around thirty years old that the newness circled back around. At a village wedding, he gave a command (at his mother's urging) and great stone jars of water suddenly overflowed with sumptuous wine (John 2:1–12). Then the healings started, the lame stood and walked, the blind opened their eyes, and the sick woke up and left their diseases and dysfunctions behind. Even the dead arose, and while the people had seen magic tricks before, this was something different that couldn't be explained away or debunked.

Jesus Becomes the News

As we see in the Gospels, the newness of what Jesus said and did became very big news, and bunches of people began to follow him. He listened to these new friends, told them stories, taught them, and prayed for them. He ate and drank with them, opened up the Scriptures and read to them in the synagogues, and cared for them. He sparred with the skeptics and accusers, and when they threw out snares and judgments, he went silent and walked away to new places.

Those in the establishment grew angry at this new kind of man. He wasn't the flavor of Messiah they were hoping for—a king with a royal bloodline, a strongman leader who would remove the yoke of the Roman Empire, or a mystical rabbi who would turn his miraculous powers toward building up the kingdom of Israel. "My kingdom is not of this world," Jesus once said (John 18:36), pushing back against these other messianic conceptions.

It turned out his stories, sermons, and prayers all pointed to a new way of life, an upside-down life where the first would be last and the last would be first. Empire and riches and military might were not his way or the way of his followers. Instead, justice and healing for the lowly and oppressed were what he cared about. Widows and orphans were more important than kings and religious leaders. Children made him smile. He noticed the misfits and the beggars, and he was drawn to these lowly ones.

Jesus's stories, sermons, and prayers all pointed to a new way of life, an upside-down life.

Finally, he'd offended and irritated so many that the Romans and the religious leaders in Jerusalem had enough, and they killed him. Crucifixion wasn't new at all, but he died quickly, surprising the Romans, and he was taken down on a Friday and put into a new stone tomb provided by a follower. On Sunday, the tomb was empty and angels were sitting nearby.

Where is his body? What have they done with him? Nothing like this has ever happened before, they must have been saying.

A New Kind of Human

Following his death and resurrection, Jesus showed up in a body made new again to a number of his disciples. He appeared to Mary Magdalene, two of his followers on the road to Emmaus, and a group of friends behind closed doors. He cooked and ate breakfast with fishermen on the shores of the Sea of Galilee, and he asked Thomas to touch his scarred hands. And he appeared to many others according to the Gospels. His last appearance on earth, which took place after he'd ascended to the heavens, was to Saul (also known as Paul). It was all new. There was no precedent for any of it.

Jesus was fully human and fully God, a new kind of being, but he didn't want to keep that sort of newness to himself. He wanted to share it, and he called it being born again. This was a radical kind of newness, and he didn't completely explain how it happened. "Humans can reproduce only human life, but the Holy Spirit gives birth to spiritual life," he said. "So don't be surprised when I say, 'You must be born again'" (John 3:6–7 NLT). Not only was Jesus new, but he offered to make others new too.

From this new life Jesus took on when he started breathing again, and from the regeneration and renewal experienced by his followers, came a new and invisible kingdom. The new kingdom was populated by a new family of believers called the church, accompanied by the promise of a new world and a new creation to come. There was to be a re-*new*-al of all things.

This was all new, and yet it wasn't. The promise of a new order, a new creation, a new king, a new kingdom, a new way of living and breathing and moving—well, it was all throughout the Old (or First) Testament. There were hints and teasers and prophecies foreshadowing the newness Jesus would bring to earth. It's just that we didn't understand it. We couldn't imagine it. It wasn't what we thought would happen or who we thought would bring this. It was all too new, like it is for visually or aurally impaired people who have corrective surgery and suddenly can see or hear, but their brains aren't used to processing this information. Although they have remade senses, they don't quite know yet how to process what they are taking in.

These remade people will "shine like the sun in the kingdom of their Father" (Matthew 13:43), and this shining like the sun is a "new newness," artist Makoto Fujimura says. The Greek word Paul uses for this state of newness is *kainos*, which is more than transformation—it's transfiguration. The way Paul uses the term is "not just a new species, but a new concept of what a species is," says Fujimura. "Paul is describing how we are a 'new [*kainos*] creation' as the resurrected Christ enters our lives."[2] This new state is so much more than a whitewash of fresh creamy paint. We are new creations, following Jesus who makes all things new.

Jesus brought a new way of living and relating to God, and we have to grapple with that, try to process it, and figure out who we are now that we are new too. We are new people together in a new kingdom, looking forward to a new world to come. And when I think about that, I feel something like I do when I look at those freshly painted kitchen cabinets—full of light and hope, seeing details I never noticed before, feeling a sense of joy and wonder. And I can't stop staring.

---

1. Do you have any skills or hobbies that can transform something old into something new? Have you ever worked on a cleanup crew after an event? How do your body and emotions respond to seeing something renewed?
2. How do you understand the phrase "my kingdom is not of this world"? What aspects of "kingdom" and "world" do you see in your local community? Where do you see Jesus's newness breaking in?
3. How have you experienced the newness of Jesus in your own life? Are there aspects of who you are that have changed over time? What aspects have stayed the same? How are you helping to renew your community?

Explore: Visit a local art museum or gallery or take in a live music performance. Reflect on how raw materials (wood, canvas, string, metal, etc.) can become creative works. Share your appreciation for the work with the artist or composer.

Chapter 4

Jesus Was the God-Human

HEATHER HART

This name is a sea, unfathomable to all thoughts, inexhaustible to all understanding, unpronounceable to all tongues, ungraspable to every spirit except the one from which it emerged. It is . . . a point from which issue all the lines, circles, angles, pictures, and figures of all our salvation's surveying.[1]

—CATHARINA REGINA VON GREIFFENBERG

The blackboard was awash with angles, shapes, and formulas. I sat with my math book open, but what I really wanted to do was smack the erasers together and shower the earth with a cloud of chalk dust. Junior high math wasn't my favorite class, but geometry had its intriguing moments. This is when I first learned about *pi*.

As a refresher, *pi* is the sixteenth letter of the Greek alphabet, and it represents the mathematical ratio of a circle's circumference to diameter. This is the distance around a circle divided by the distance across it. You may remember it as 3.14159 . . . , but understanding this concept sent a bit of a shock wave to the orderly, concrete number side of my brain. Here was a ratio, true for all circles, that was an infinite number. It did not resolve into an integer. It was "irrational." *Pi* is consistent and useful in formulas, but it is not a tidy whole number. I can never get to the end of it.

Trying to define "divinity joined to humanity" feels a bit irrational, like a number I can never fully wrap my mind around. The reality that Jesus is the God-human is not an easily manageable concept. My finite human descriptions are insufficient, but sorting through the complexity of the idea of God-human helps me understand who God is, what he has done, and how I relate to him.

God is not like me. God is one being in three persons, and one of those persons has two natures: an eternal divine nature and a human nature. I am one being—one person with one human nature. God will always be beyond me, yet God came near to me and all of humanity through Jesus. God's willingness to come near, be embodied, and join in humanity demonstrates love, power, and compassion in the most personal way possible.

Divinity Joined Humanity

The Gospels give us a picture of Jesus as both divine and human. The first chapter of the gospel of John begins with an echo of Genesis 1:1 with the phrase "In the beginning," and then calls Jesus "the Word." John 1:1 declares, "The Word was with God, and the Word was God" (NRSVue). The gospel continues in verse 14 with: "The Word became flesh and lived among us." The eternally divine Word joined with humanity in Jesus. In similar fashion, Paul's letters repeatedly take one of the Old Testament names for the divine being, *Lord* (*kyrios* in Greek), and use it as the title for Jesus.[2] Paul assumes Jesus's humanity and divinity. He doesn't offer an argument for it; he simply begins with the reality that Jesus is God and then describes how believers should live. These New Testament writings show us a new level of complexity concerning who God is. God is still loving, powerful, and compassionate, but now Jesus gives deeper insight into the workings of divinity.[3]

In the fourth century, the church worked to articulate this complexity in the Nicene Creed. This creed poetically describes Jesus's eternal divinity as "the only-begotten Son of God, begotten of the Father before all the ages, Light of Light, true God of true God, begotten not made, of one substance with the Father, through whom all things were made." His embodied humanity "was made flesh of the Holy Spirit and the Virgin Mary and became man."[4] The God of the Old Testament and Jesus are not different in substance, power, or importance. The Word has always existed, but through the Holy Spirit working in Mary, the Word became human. One divine person now had two natures and a human body.

To Be with Humanity

God has always wanted to be near humanity. The creation story shows us God's care and desire to be with humanity. The separation that came after Eve and Adam ate the fruit was not part of God's original relational design. God's desire to be with humanity did not change, but human rebellion fractured what had once been good. In this context of a fractured relationship, the Word becoming flesh in Jesus takes on layers of significance.

> The name Jesus is the glow of love, the desire of salvation, the sea of sweetness, and the land of the living, a foretaste of heaven, and the quintessence of all good deeds of Christ.[5]

We long for more than what surrounds us. This world wobbles on an axis of suffering, and we wonder who can right it. Because of the separation between God and humanity, we humans cannot bring goodness into the world on our own. Human goodness is a result of being connected to God and spreading God's goodness. The fractured relationship between God and humanity means we are caught in a self-perpetuating cycle of brokenness. Humanity's cooperation in expanding God's good rule ("dominion" in Genesis 1:26) is not realized in the world around us. The pain, destruction, and death of this world are unmistakable. Jesus's human nature declares that God has entered directly into that pain, destruction, and death in order to overturn it and begin a rebirth. God becoming human means that on our own, we cannot save ourselves. We are helpless to change our circumstances. We need someone to save us. We need God to take decisive action. God's decisive action begins in the God-human, Jesus.[6]

Because Jesus has two natures—God and human—divinity and humanity are now connected. This connection is passed along to all who follow Jesus and are transformed by him. Jesus, the true Son of God, brings us into the family of God. We are no longer separated; a renewed closeness is possible for humanity. Jesus becomes the new Adam, the source for humanity, transforming us from a lineage perpetuating rebellion into a lineage cooperating with God. By entering a disordered, chaotic, and fallen world and refusing to be corrupted by it, Jesus fundamentally reorders this world.[7] Corruption will not stand; it has begun to crumble.

To Bring About Renewal

On the cross, Jesus remained fully divine and fully human. This means that his eternal divine nature remained in union with the Father and the Holy Spirit.[8] The Trinity continued unbroken. Jesus's two natures are not two different persons, so Jesus's humanity was not abandoned by God on the cross either. Jesus's experience of being forsaken relates to his suffering and death. The Father could have rescued Jesus from suffering and death but did not.[9] Jesus's human nature went through suffering and death because he identifies with us and stands in for us, and because a corrupt world cannot tolerate true faithfulness to God.[10] Jesus identified with our humanity. He took the results of sin on our behalf and exemplified allegiance to God above all. Jesus's actions are for our salvation. Jesus chose this path not because suffering is good but because of the joy set before him: God's good plan to renew creation will move forward.

For this renewal, humanity looks to Jesus as the ultimate example. Jesus experienced a fully human life, knowing brokenness and temptation. He demonstrated how humanity is to live in the power of the Holy Spirit. Jesus lived his human life perfectly because the Spirit empowered and directed him. Followers of Jesus learn to live according to the Spirit and are transformed into new humanity.[11] This requires cooperation between us and the Spirit. Our desire for salvation is initiated and enabled by the Spirit, and ultimately the Spirit shapes us to be people like Jesus.

Jesus chose this path not because suffering is good but because of the joy set before him.

Jesus is the God-human because we cannot save ourselves, and God's plan to partner with humanity in spreading goodness through the earth meant his taking on human flesh through the life and work of his Son. But what does it mean to reorder our lives around this truth, that God came to earth to do something important, something that needed doing? First, it means you're not imagining things when the world around you looks broken and corrupt. It *is* broken and corrupt, but the renewal has begun in Jesus. God knows you and the pain in your world. God has entered into it personally. Jesus declares you are worth saving.

Second, it means that it is not on your shoulders to fix this world. Jesus is the renewal, not you. He wants you to join in and cooperate with this renewal, but you are not meant to sacrifice yourself on the altar for humanity. Jesus has already done that. When you see God working, then join in with your whole being, but sleep at night and take Sabbath rest knowing it ultimately depends on God, not you.

Third, it means that when you connect with Jesus, you are part of God's family. You are included. Even if you have no earthly family or have felt devastating rejection, Jesus has opened a new relational path for you. Family now takes on a new meaning; it is expanded far beyond biology or legal rights. You belong in God's family.

Fourth, it means connecting your lineage through Jesus will transform you. You will be made new; the devastation of being in Adam's line is undone. This transformation is neither coercive nor circumvented. It is patient and loving. Yet this is not merely a matter of conforming behaviors. Jesus is after a transformation of your very humanity. The Spirit will make you into the image of God that you were intended to be. Following Jesus always transforms us in the power of the Spirit.

Fifth, it means that the renewal of all of creation has begun—a revolution is underway. The old order of things is ending and a new order has begun. This world is not fully renewed; corruption and death still exist. But goodness has broken into this world decisively, and it will triumph.

Finally, it means that Jesus loves you. Jesus loves humanity. God did not turn away from suffering and death but entered into it. You are able to turn toward others mired in suffering and death and point them toward Jesus. You can point them toward the God-human who loves them and remains faithful.

You do not need to have all the complexities of Jesus's two natures ironed out; there will always be a mystery to divinity. We don't need to resolve *pi* for it to be meaningful. We follow Jesus and trust the Spirit to renew us. Through the Spirit you will know Jesus, the God-human, who brings us our only salvation. His arms are wide open.

---

1. What faith concepts have been difficult for you to understand? Have you found any metaphors that help you grasp difficult aspects of Christianity?

2. How were you taught about Jesus's divine and human natures? Was one side emphasized more than the other? Is there a particular aspect of Jesus's two natures that you prefer to meditate on?
3. How comfortable are you with the idea of divine mystery? Does your faith community allow space for unresolved complexity? Does this feel comforting or like a shortcut?

Explore: Make a list of some spiritual concepts that you find complex or unresolved. The book *Practicing Christian Doctrine* by Beth Felker Jones can offer helpful insight into ideas like the Trinity and salvation. Reflect on how your body and emotions respond to hearing different viewpoints.

Chapter 5

Jesus Was Dependent

AMANDA WEBER

Jesus gave them this answer: "Very truly I tell you, the Son can do nothing by himself; he can do only what he sees his Father doing, because whatever the Father does the Son also does."
—JOHN 5:19

Max trots into the kitchen, turns, and stares at me with his gleaming caramel eyes. I continue wiping down the counters, rinse out the cloth, and hang it over the oven handle to dry. When I turn around, our fluffy three-year-old cockapoo is still holding me in his gaze, eager to see whether I will head toward the back door or over to the couch. Is it time to play ball, or is it time for a nap? Since Max adores me, he usually seems fine either way; he just wants to be right by my side. Plus, as my son likes to remind my daughter when it's her turn to feed the dog, Max lacks opposable thumbs. So as smart as he is, there is a lot that we must do for him. If I've decided we're going outside, I turn the doorknob and we both go through the door. If it's time for dinner, I scoop out his kibble for him and he eats. I provide the direction and the power that he lacks. I am attentive to his needs and see that they are met. He brings himself, his canine affection, and eagerness to join me wherever I go.

Max reminds me how creation can vividly reflect our Creator and demonstrate profound truths within the confines of everyday life. When Jesus commenced his ministry in human flesh, he took every opportunity to emphasize that he looked to the Father to see what he is doing and then joined him. Likewise, he depended on the power of the Spirit to carry out God's mission. Much of Christian faith and practice is built on the premise that the most fulfilling life is one lived in humble dependence on God. Any other way of life is just pretending. It should not surprise us, then, that Jesus beautifully modeled this dependence on God as a loving means of redemption, showing solidarity and revealing his goodness.

Dependence and Interdependence

Before going further, I need to address the elephant in the room. Isn't Jesus God? And isn't God supposed to be all-powerful? If someone is dependent, doesn't that mean they have a need that they *can't* meet on their own? Is saying that Jesus was dependent the kind of statement that could get us burned at the stake (or fried on Facebook) for heresy? How human was Jesus really? Isn't saying that he was dependent a little too human for comfort? And by "too human," don't we mean flawed? These are unsettling questions! Any honest theologian will tell you that the manner by which Jesus was both fully God and fully human remains a mystery to the human mind. But Christians' best efforts at explaining it hinge on two fancy Greek words: *kenosis* and *perichoresis*.

It is true that Christian tradition has established that God *is* supremely powerful and *not* subject to limitations by any outside force in the way the rest of creation is.[1] But God has chosen to *self-impose* limitations in order to reveal himself and enable redemption and communion with humanity. The mere fact of the incarnation demonstrates this point, as Jesus suspends dependence upon his divine powers and takes on human flesh. *Kenosis* is a Greek word that theologians adopted to describe this mystery (Philippians 2:7). But in accepting embodiment as a male *homo sapiens* in a specific geographical and historical moment, Jesus does not "play chicken" with God's plans. Rather, he relies on the other persons of the Trinity—the Father and the Holy Spirit—just as God designed the rest of humanity to do always. This beautiful and dynamic union without loss of particularity among the persons of the Trinity is known as *perichoresis*.

Dependence Reveals Connection

Kenosis and *perichoresis* are big words for fuzzy concepts. Here is another way to think about it: Jesus is God's self-portrait within human flesh. When we observe Jesus, we learn about God's character and discover how God intends us to connect with him. One of the first scriptural accounts we have of Jesus is at his baptism. In choosing to be baptized, Jesus modeled an appropriate human response to God. He welcomed God's powerful cleansing, renewing Spirit to flow through him. Matthew's narration of this event captures my heart with his description of God's uniquely loving and interdependent nature (3:13–17). As Jesus rises from the water, the Holy Spirit descends upon him in the form of a dove, signaling the kingly anointing of the presence and peace of God. Father God announces to onlookers that Jesus is his Son, whom he loves and in whom he delights! Jesus doesn't need to trumpet his legitimacy and authority; the Father does it for him. Love and honor are reciprocal within this relationship. The Father trusts the Son with his teaching and ministry of justice, peace, reconciliation, healing, and resurrection.

Jesus is God's self-portrait within human flesh.

Later, when Jesus talks about doing God's works, his divinity and the authority that coincides with doing the Father's will seem to grow more evident.[2] The kingdom of God always looks like a way of life where God lovingly reigns and rules. Jesus lived this and taught his disciples to pray in a Father-centric way: "Our Father . . . your will be done" (6:9–10). Anyone who witnessed Jesus's baptism and knew the ancient Scriptures would have seen this regular, dripping wet man in a totally different light. This is the promised Davidic king and Messiah, the one who would rescue God's people from exile and restore justice and peace to the land! In this glorious scene, all the persons of the Trinity work in concert to reveal the nature and means of God's salvation. God is faithful to save, and humans are enabled to depend fully on God.

Jesus: The Example of Dependency

After his baptism, Jesus does not act or look like a Superman-type hero, except for the fact that he heads straight into a confrontation with evil. How does God win victories against evil? Whether God's people are many or few, God conquers evil "not by might nor by power, but by my Spirit" (Zechariah 4:6). Now the Holy Spirit leads Jesus into the wilderness. Similar ancient wilderness stories in the Old Testament often describe times of transformation, preparation, or proofing for the heroes' future mission. In Jesus's wilderness experience, he relived, or at least evoked, Israel's experience of Yahweh leading them through a time of testing and trust building through the wilderness after the exodus to make them ready to receive and live in their prosperous destiny. But the Israelites failed. They did not live in the way of wisdom but instead broke trust with God time and again.

Even after moving into the promised land, the people of God worshipped other gods and decided what to do by looking at their powerful neighbors instead of their God. They were not content with Yahweh as their King; they wanted a trendy human ruler. But none of these mortal kings—not even God's favored David—could deliver what the people needed to make them whole. Whereas the Israelites failed to contentedly rest in God's leadership and provision, Jesus embodied and exemplified faithfulness to God. He refused temptations to take up the glory, exaltation, and self-direction that rightfully belonged to him, as this would cut short his incarnational ministry. Jesus knew his calling was to continue representing dependence on the Father and the Spirit for all who needed a new vision of who they could—and would—be in him.

After Jesus's death and resurrection, he comforts all who love him with the knowledge that God's presence remains among us in the person of the Spirit. We are all invited to experience that unique, livening, and renewing fellowship with God in Jesus's style of dependence. Indeed, the church is meant to be a community marked by dependence on God and interdependence among one another. Each of us, no matter how weak, is gifted by the Holy Spirit for our mutual good. None of us can say we don't need each other.

Today I need a new vision for what it means to depend on God and to experience interdependence in community, treacherous and broken as we are. I love to feel independent and often struggle to respect people who seem needy. In my more authentic moments, I suspect this is because I am all too aware of my own lack of superhuman powers and am unaccustomed to depending on God on behalf of others. "Practicing Christlike dependence" is not a common topic for small groups, leadership conferences, or sermons (not in my circles at least). Perhaps a life of dependence on God starts with the relieved assurance that God knows I don't have the divine equivalent of opposable thumbs, and he doesn't expect me to grow them. Somehow, like Max and like Jesus, I have to trust that doors will open and food will be provided as I keep returning to Jesus's example, praying, "Our Father who art in heaven," and responding to the Spirit however I am able at the time. This is faith.

---

1. How were you taught to value independence, dependence, and interdependence as a child? Has your understanding of them changed in adulthood?

2. Who do you know that demonstrates dependence on God? What does their dependence look like in daily activities? Do they ever express fear or uncertainty or doubt?
3. What might it feel like to be considered "needy" in your faith community? In what ways do you see interdependence demonstrated in your church?

Explore: Write out a list of ways you depend on God and ways you are interdependent in your faith community. Where do these lists overlap?

Chapter 6

Jesus Was a Student

AMANDA CLARK

Jesus grew in wisdom.
—LUKE 2:52

When my husband Justin and I got married, one of the first tough decisions we had to make was which of our churches we would attend. He won, and I have never regretted our choice. We loved that church, made enduring friendships there, and most of all, sat under the teaching of a brilliant pastor. Kent was the first person I had ever known who was seminary educated, and he had put his education to work as an engaging Bible teacher.

But as a twenty-year-old not pursuing higher education, I did not attribute Kent's excellent grasp of Scripture to his education and ongoing study of the Word; I just thought he was a genius. I was amazed at how much he knew, but I did not connect the dots to the hours spent in commentaries and his well-worn Greek dictionary. Kent did have a good mind, but he knew what he knew because he studied the work of scholars and theologians.

Fast-forward sixteen years and I am in my first year of pastoring, preaching most weekends and trying to keep up with my seminary studies. One day I was having a conversation with a young adult member of the church when they exclaimed, "I think you're *soooo* smart, and I don't understand how you know so much about the Bible!" I quickly set the record straight. "I know things you might not know about the Bible because I am in school, and I'm preaching what I'm learning, but no, it doesn't come naturally. I work my tail off to write good sermons." I chuckle now at the pedestal I had put Kent on, because I know now that he wasn't a Bible superhero. He was a student.

Shouldn't Jesus Already Know It All?

Similarly, many people have never considered that Jesus was a student. They assume that Jesus's incredible miracles, along with his brilliant understanding and interpretation of the law, just came naturally because he was the Son of God. In every announcement of the arrival of the kingdom of God, in every retort to the Pharisees, in every allusion to or recitation of the Old Testament Scriptures, the common belief is that Jesus simply knew everything.

But when Jesus became human, he was no longer able to know everything all at once. Philippians 2:6–7 says that Jesus, "though he existed in the form of God, did not regard equality with God as something to be grasped, but emptied himself" (NRSVue). When Jesus became human, he was fully God, but in order to become fully human, he gave up the exercise of his divine attributes. This means he could not be everywhere at once as God—such as hanging out with his mother in Nazareth while walking the dirt roads around Galilee with Peter and Andrew at the same time—but was limited to the constraints of the human body. He did not have knowledge of everything that would happen in world history, and if you had handed him an iPhone, he wouldn't have known how to install an app any better than your grandma. If Jesus had retained his divine qualities, such as the ability to know all things or to be in all places at once, he would have been a superhuman. We can't do those things, so if Jesus had been able to, he would not have been fully human.

In contrast to this image of Jesus as a superhuman, Luke's gospel gives a lot of clues to us that Jesus's power—such as his ability to sometimes read thoughts (5:22; 6:8; 9:47; 11:17), to heal (5:24–25; 6:10), and to raise the dead (7:11–17)—came from the power of the Holy Spirit (3:22; 4:1, 14; 5:17; 10:21). Jesus was formed in Mary by the power of the Holy Spirit (1:35), Jesus received the indwelling Holy Spirit at the moment of his baptism (3:22) and was "full of the Holy Spirit" (4:1) from that moment on. It does seem as though Jesus experienced a greater measure of the Holy Spirit than most Jesus followers do, possibly because his ability to hear from the Spirit was not hampered by personal struggle with sin. But Jesus was not a superhuman; he was human, and as a human, he had to learn.

Learning as a Child

A remarkable element of the Christian faith is that our Scriptures present a God who loved us so much that God became one of us. In the incarnation, Jesus did not come to earth as a full-grown and self-aware Messiah. No, Matthew and Luke tell us of a Jesus who was born an infant, like any other infant, and had to learn everything a normal human child learns—to speak, to walk, to eat without assistance, to obey his parents. He was not born with a complete knowledge of the Hebrew Scriptures or of his calling and mission; he had to learn them.

Jesus had to learn from the same people and institutions from which any child learns: from his family and his community. His parents would have been the ones to teach him his ABCs and 123s, to use a phrase from our day.[1] Jesus appears to have known how to read (Luke 4:16), and it is possible that his father gave him vocational training in the carpentry trade.

Unfortunately, the gospel accounts tell us almost nothing about Jesus's childhood except for one relevant account in Luke 2:41–52. In this passage, Jesus travels to Jerusalem with his parents for a Jewish festival, but when his parents finally leave the Jerusalem temple, he stays behind. When his family finally find him, they discover that he has been captivating the teachers at the temple for three days, asking questions and engaging with them, such that "all who heard him were amazed at his understanding and his answers" (verse 47 NRSVue). Jesus's parents were frantic and upset with him, but his twelve-year-old mind simply waved it off, as if they ought to have known he would be tending to his Father's interests. Yes, the sages were amazed at his understanding, but we still ought not think of this as a boy Jesus with superhuman wisdom and knowledge. Luke's emphasis seems to be the idea that Jesus at age twelve was beginning to come into self-understanding. His relationship with the Father was unique, and perhaps in this visit to the temple, along with a keen interest in the Torah, he was putting some of the puzzle pieces together.

Jesus was not born with a complete knowledge of the Hebrew Scriptures or of his calling and mission; he had to learn them.

Jesus's first teacher, along with his education in Torah, was likely his mother. Mary seems to have influenced the first two chapters of Luke's gospel,[2] and what we learn of her understanding of Jesus's destiny was probably passed to Jesus and then worked out in his mind. After the temple incident, Luke tells us that Jesus went home and was obedient to his parents. Jesus would have learned of his miraculous birth and the events surrounding it from his parents and most intimately from Mary. Indeed, Luke makes a point to tell us that Mary "treasured up all these things and pondered them in her heart" (2:19), which means she herself was working through all the implications of her son's unparalleled calling. New Testament scholar Richard Bauckham says of Jesus's preministry years, "Evidently, Jesus will have much to think and work through *with her* concerning his mission."[3] Mary was the first disciple of Jesus, but Jesus was a student of Mary.

Jesus Never Stopped Learning

We also know that Jesus continued being a student in his adulthood by attending synagogues and learning from the teachers of the law. Before Jesus began his public ministry, he had been a member of the synagogue in Nazareth. Mentions of his visits to the synagogue during his early ministry indicate that Jesus didn't just go to receive an opportunity to speak but also because he was a faithful attender. However, whatever Jesus learned from others, by the time he began his ministry, the Holy Spirit empowered him with authority to teach notably different from other teachers (Matthew 7:29).

God was willing to become human and put himself in the humbling position of learning from the people he had created. Jesus sets an example for us of lifelong learning and a posture of humility. As a frequently overwhelmed seminary student and brand-new pastor, I find both inspiration and comfort in the fact that like me, Jesus had to apply himself and learn. From his position as the highest and greatest, Jesus was a student.

---

1. What was your experience in school like? How has your past experience with learning shaped your present-day questions about faith?
2. How does your local community view spiritual curiosity? What about spiritual confusion or spiritual doubt?
3. What aspects of your faith would you like to learn more about? Has anyone recognized a particular spiritual gifting in you that should be further developed? What would that development look like?

Explore: Think about one or two close friends and reflect on their spiritual gifting. Write them a note describing how you see God's gifting in their life and encourage their further development.

Chapter 7

Jesus Was Not White

SHEVA STEPHENS KNOTT

So God created human beings in his own image.
In the image of God he created them;
male and female he created them.
—Genesis 1:27 (NLT)

My grandmother had three photos I viewed as a child, three images that shaped my environment, brought me comfort, and served as a North Star, of sorts, for my own sense of identity. Those images have been a part of my life ever since: a photo of Dr. Martin Luther King Jr., a photo of Malcolm X, and a popular portrait of a blond-haired, blue-eyed Jesus.

Images can tell a story, shape a cultural climate, and evoke emotions of all sorts. They can illumine truths that liberate hearts, minds, and lives, and they can perpetuate falsehoods that bind them. Some images do all these things. So it has been with that famous Jesus picture of my childhood. For millions of Christians, this photo (officially entitled *Head of Christ*) has been a conduit of grace. For countless others, including me, it reflects something far different.

In the formative years of my faith, the striking differences between this portrait of Jesus and the pictures of Dr. King and Malcolm X caused an internal conflict for me. That Western European image of

Jesus did not reconcile with my own internal image of the Jesus I had prayed to and studied. Rather, it catalyzed my journey away from the local church with a faith-shaking question: How can a Jesus who looks like that identify with the image I see in the mirror?

Seeing Pictures of Jesus

Head of Christ, also known as the "Sallman Head," originated as a charcoal sketch by artist Warner Sallman, who called it *Son of Man*. The artwork was created in 1924 for the cover of the *Covenant Companion*, the denominational magazine for the Evangelical Covenant Church. Over the years, several reproductions of Sallman's artwork have been created. In 1935, for example, a version composed in oil paint was created for the fiftieth-anniversary celebration of the Evangelical Covenant Church. Sallman's *Head of Christ* presents an obviously Northern European Jesus featuring blue eyes, auburn hair, and pale skin. Sallman's painting stood in stark contrast to other paintings of Jesus depicting a dark-skinned Jewish Jesus, such as Rembrandt's *Head of Christ* (1650).[1]

Sallman's inspiration for his sketch came as a miraculous answer to prayer, per his own account: "The answer came at 2 A.M., January 1924. . . . A sign. An answered prayer. It came as a vision in response to my prayer to God in a despairing situation."[2] The miracle for Sallman was meeting his deadline for the *Covenant Companion*. While his faith led Sallman to create artwork of Jesus, his employment in advertising caused the focus to be on "what kind of face would most appeal to a large and diverse audience of twentieth-century consumers."[3] The advertisement achieved its end result with the picture receiving widespread acceptance.

The picture has become the basis for millions of people's visualization of Jesus, and remarkable stories have been associated with it. These include people making deathbed confessions upon seeing the image, thieves aborting their misdeeds in the presence of the portrait, or even the eyes of Christ weeping when viewed by a boy with leukemia, who afterward was declared miraculously free of his affliction. This last encounter has inspired annual pilgrimages to view the painting. Such is its power, but therein also lies its problem.

For all the devotion that inspired Sallman to create his art, his depiction of a fair-skinned, Westernized Jesus hardly resembles the historical Jesus, a dark-complected Jewish man of Mediterranean origins. And so there are two sides to *The Head of Christ*. For one person, it can represent hope and salvific life. But for another, it has the opposite effect. It perpetuates a deeply entrenched mindset that conforms Jesus to the image and likeness of the stereotypical white, North Atlantic male and, by extension, relegates peoples of other appearances and cultures to second-class status and represents oppression.

Sallman's artificial, ethereal-looking construct of Jesus as a Caucasian man fails to embody the physical reality of the historical "man of sorrows, acquainted with deepest grief" (Isaiah 53:3 NLT), who knew firsthand the injustices, struggles, and heartaches of those outside the ruling class. Indeed, that blue-eyed image looks very much like our country's (predominately white) ruling class. It looks nothing like the vast majority of the world's population. More than seven billion of us are "painted out" of this iconic image.[4] And that is a travesty. *The Head of Christ* doesn't resemble the historical Savior of the whole world.

To put it simply, Jesus was not white.

Race and Identity

The Bible says nothing about Jesus's skin tone when he walked the earth. But no evidence supports his belonging to the white race, much less to any "race." Race, as we think about it, is a modern-day invention. Our emphasis on skin color as the defining characteristic of race began with Europe's exploration of the Americas and Africa. However, in antiquity (the Greco-Roman world) skin color was negligible in defining race.[5]

Race is a shorthand term used to describe and categorize people in various social groups based on skin color, physical features, and genetic heredity. It is not a valid biological concept. Rather, race is a social construction that gives or denies benefits and privileges, with damaging consequences for the underdogs. David Roediger states in his book *How Race Survived US History*, "The world got along without race for the overwhelming majority of its history. The US has never been without it."[6]

Historically, people have been identified in relation to geographical identifiers, family lineage, or the culture they were a part of. Jesus is no different. He was identified not by his physical traits but by

Geography: "And because Joseph [Jesus's 'stepfather'] was a descendant of King David, he had to go to Bethlehem in Judea, David's ancient home. He traveled there from the village of Nazareth in Galilee" (Luke 2:4 NLT). Bethlehem is where Joseph and Jesus's mother, Mary, would travel to be counted in the census ordered by Caesar Augustus for the entire Roman Empire.

Lineage: In Micah 5:2, the prophet writes,

> But you, Bethlehem Ephrathah,
>   though you are small among the clans of Judah,
> out of you will come for me
>   one who will be ruler over Israel,
> whose origins are from of old,
>   from ancient times.

Culture: Matthew records that the Magi asked, "Where is the one who has been born *king of the Jews*? We saw his star when it rose and have come to worship him" (2:2).

There is no record in Scripture that speaks to the skin color of Jesus. True, Revelation 1:14–15 describes Christ's appearance in detail, with white hair, eyes like flames, feet like bronze, and a voice like ocean waves. But that is a vision of Jesus in his glory. No person on earth fits that description.

So what did Jesus and his Judean neighbors look like? Realistically, they had brown skin. The biblical towns that Jesus encounters in the Gospels—Bethlehem, Nazareth, Capernaum, and Jerusalem, among others—were all located in a region populated by people of color. One of them was Jesus's mother. Mary was a brown woman, and she gave birth to a brown baby who grew up into a brown man. Jesus's skin tone was a natural result of his geography. Brown was normal in Judea during the Roman period, and normal was a good thing during a ministry that was controversial enough as it stood.

The Images We Create

Warner Sallman's intentions were not ignoble. He believed the image he first rendered as a charcoal sketch was the answer to his heartfelt faith. And his creation, *The Head of Christ*, has brought hope and peace to many people across the world. But an artist cannot guarantee how his work will be received. Images have an innate ambiguity that can support an interpretive narrative that stands in complete contrast with the artist's intent. *The Head of Christ* is an example of this. By portraying Jesus as a blue-eyed, light-skinned male, *The Head of Christ* has conditioned millions to imagine Jesus as a white man instead of as the dark-skinned Middle Eastern man he actually was.

Mary was a brown woman, and she gave birth to a brown baby who grew up into a brown man.

As historical constructs are being dismantled, the fallacy of a white Jesus needs to go. Jesus was not white. Embracing this truth expands, not reduces, Jesus's impact. It restores him to his proper position as the one who identified with the oppressed and who empowered them to follow and be free; the one who, defying the brutal Roman Empire, showed his followers that no king is greater than the King of Kings; and the one who taught that to support the community is the greatest thing of all.

The late great Dr. E. V. Hill was once asked if he thought Jesus was white, as depicted in paintings. This was his reply:

> I don't know anything about a white Jesus. . . . I know about Christ, a Savior named Jesus. I don't know what color He is. He was born in the brown Middle East; He fled to black Africa, and He was in heaven before the gospel got to white Europe. So, I don't know what color He is.
>
> I do know one thing: if you bow at the altar with color on your mind, you'll get up with color on your mind. Go back again—and keep going back until you no longer look at His color, but at His greatness and His power—His power to save![7]

I was raised in a house where three figures helped shape and guide my life. While the image of Jesus Christ—white, blond, and blue-eyed—belonged to an earlier time, it helped women like me—who descended from generations of slavery, Jim Crow, reconstruction, and civil rights eras—hold on to hope. But I also found hope in the freedom to question that image and to then be guided by the Word of God, the Holy Bible. It is in this questioning that I was able to reconcile Jesus with the image I see in the mirror.

Over the years I returned to my grandmother's home often and sought to note differences and continuity between Jesus our hope and salvation and the Jesus of *The Head of Christ*. You see, over time the image of the blond, blue-eyed Jesus disappeared from sight. Over coffee and old Mahalia Jackson records, my grandmother and I started learning about the Jesus of the Bible. The Jesus of hope. The Jesus of grace and mercy. The Jesus of diversity and inclusion. The Jesus who is "I AM WHO I AM" (Exodus 3:14 NLT) and who makes himself available to all.

---

1. Did you grow up around images of Jesus (e.g., pictures, children's Bibles, Sunday school materials)? If so, describe those images and how you've understood their meaning over the years.
2. How does it affect your body and emotions to think about Jesus as a man with brown skin?
3. Who in your community could benefit from seeing and hearing descriptions of Jesus as a non-white Savior?

Explore: Find and read a book that depicts Jesus with a more historically accurate skin tone. Reflect on how you feel. A good example is *Picturing the Bible: The Earliest Christian Art* by Jeffrey Spier (Kimbell Art Museum, 2008).

Chapter 8

Jesus Was a Barrier Breaker

TERRI FULLERTON

> *"Love the Lord your God with all your heart and with all your soul and with all your mind and with all your strength." The second is this: "Love your neighbor as yourself." There is no commandment greater than these.*
>
> —Mark 12:30–31

I remember looking up at one of the ladies in our Bible study as her tear-filled eyes revealed the news was not what we had prayed for—namely, that she would find favor with the judge. She was one of many women who showed up weekly for a Bible study at a prison for those incarcerated for lacking proper immigration documentation.

Through a translator we discovered the ruling was deportation to Guatemala, the country where she was born, the next morning. Her parents had fled in the night when she was two months old. She had no memory of the country. Her parents, siblings, spouse, and children were here, but out of fear, no family members visited her in the detention facility.

That evening, with a smaller group than usual, we ended our lesson circled around her. We took turns praying in our own languages for her and her family. Our tears communicated our groans. We walked out silenced by the grief of injustice in a complicated system of immigration.

On the way home that night, I thought about the first time I'd gone to help with the Bible study an hour outside of town. Scenes of inmates in movies ran through my mind. After first meeting the women, I felt deeply sorry for the limited understanding I had of the detainees and what they had been through. Even still, I wrestle with shame and anger when I hear narratives in the media and from politicians that make non-white Americans, like the ladies in my Bible study, the dangerous "other."

When the women filed in my first night there, hugging me before sitting down, those costly assumptions evaporated. I saw Jesus in these grieving sisters and in our shared humanity. Though the ministry is long gone, it still shapes my understanding of what it means to be in the unified and diverse family of God. It expands my view of Jesus and his mission.

In the New Testament, we see how Jesus broke the socially constructed barriers of the first century and interacted with those widely viewed as undesirable or dangerous. He crossed cultural boundaries that divided humanity by ethnicity, wealth, gender, and level of practiced piety. He went to the people and places that made up the marginalized and the outcast. The movement led by Jesus embraced no hierarchy, no power over others, and no privilege.

Jesus crossed cultural boundaries that divided humanity.

In the gospel stories Jesus goes from town to town proclaiming the good news that the kingdom of heaven is near (Matthew 4:17). He not only proclaims this good news, but he also teaches and lives out what it looks like to participate in God's kingdom on earth. Don't think of the monarchy from *The Crown* here—God's kingdom isn't one of political or national subjugation. The ancient Jewish people understood the idea of "kingdom" in terms of who reigned and had authority. In the New Testament Gospels, the notion of the kingdom of heaven encompasses a way of living as Jesus's faithful witnesses that lines up with his values. According to Jesus, this way of living requires a heart of mercy (Matthew 5:7), compassion (9:35–38), forgiveness (Luke 6:37), justice (Matthew 23:23), and peace and restoration (Luke 2:14) for all. Living out the kingdom of God disrupts social, racial, ethnic, political, and national divisions.

The apostle Paul also warned of the danger of division in his letters to the churches in Ephesus, Rome, Colossae, and Galatia, exhorting them about the specific divisions that threatened to tear those communities apart.[1] In Ephesians, Paul wrote, "In his flesh he has made both [Jew and non-Jew] into one and has broken down the dividing wall, that is, the hostility between us" (2:14 NRSVue). Jesus embodies the new kingdom, God's kingdom.

Glimpses of the New Kingdom

As Jesus moved about Galilee, he showed quick glimpses of what it meant to break down walls. In Matthew after Jesus teaches the Sermon on the Mount, he comes down the hillside with crowds following him. It is then that a man with leprosy kneels before him and says, "Lord, if you are willing, you can make me clean" (8:2). Jesus already had earned a reputation as a prolific healer, so the leper likely didn't doubt Jesus's capability to heal him, but he wasn't sure Jesus would want to cure him. Under the Jewish law, people with skin diseases were isolated from the community (Leviticus 13:45–46). They were viewed as "unclean," and anyone who touched them would also become impure. But Jesus heals the leper through touch and restores him—as well as many others with diseases that led to isolation—back to life in the community.

In another example, Jesus enters Capernaum when a centurion asks him for help. The centurions were commanders in the Roman army and a manifestation of Roman tyranny; with the Jewish people living under a heavy weight of abusive taxation and oppression, this conversation must have been jarring to Jesus's disciples. Approaching Jesus, the centurion says, "Lord, . . . my servant lies at home paralyzed, suffering terribly" (Matthew 8:6). Jesus offers to go to his home, but the Roman official replies that he knows Jesus only needs to speak the command and his servant will be healed. Jesus is amazed at his understanding, exclaiming, "I have not found anyone in Israel with such great faith" (verse 10).

After healing many people in yet another crowd, Jesus gets in a boat with his disciples to cross the Sea of Galilee to a predominantly Gentile place, the region of the Gadarenes, where Jesus reveals more of his identity. When he arrives on the other side, two demon-possessed men living in tombs meet him. Again, we see Jesus unhindered by Jewish laws that would call for distance. The demons recognize him and ask the Son of God whether he is going to torture them before their time is up. In this strange story, Matthew shows us more healing and restoration to community as well as foreshadows one of the missions of Jesus: to destroy the power of evil. What kind of man is this? He is Emmanuel, *God with us*, who comes to lay down his life to stop evil, so that no one will perish. He breaks barriers to heal what has so often been fractured so that we can live, through his Spirit, as restored image bearers who point to a loving, inclusive, and righteous God.

Time and time again, Jesus healed the sick and the lame, gave sight to the blind, released those who were oppressed, provided food for the hungry, and raised the countenance of those who had a "spirit of despair" (Isaiah 61:3), fulfilling the words of the prophet Isaiah. In the Old Testament we see how God gave the Israelites instructions to love the one, true God and love their neighbors. But over and over they failed to live this out in word and deed. God's message of salvation, restoration, and healing was rooted in the covenant between God and

Abraham, serving as a light to all nations so that all peoples might know God and his salvific love for humanity. To fully grasp Jesus's teachings, mercy, and compassion, "we must realize that deep in our orientations of our spirit we cannot have one posture toward God and a different one toward other people. We are a whole being, and our true character pervades everything we do."[2]

Jesus wasn't just doing something new to be first or best. Instead, he crossed barriers to bring healing and unity, ushering in the kingdom of God on earth so that we, too, can be Christ's peace-making presence. We can show others who God is by how we love them in word and deed, even if they sit behind heavy locked doors and cold metal bars.

---

1. How did your body and emotions respond to reading the opening story? What social barriers keep people separated in your local community?
2. How does your local community respond to stories about these types of barriers? How does your church talk about unity and healing? Does your community welcome refugees?
3. What could unity look like if local barriers were removed? What would it cost you (social status, wealth, etc.) to participate in unifying your community?

Explore: Read a story of someone who has encountered significant legal and social barriers, such as *Everything Sad Is Untrue* by Daniel Nayeri or *We Were Illegal* by Jessica Goudeau. Reflect on how you feel reading these books and what you learned about this situation.

Chapter 9

Jesus Was a Winemaker, Part One

AMANDA WEBER

I have trodden the winepress alone.
—ISAIAH 63:3 (KJV)

"Christ's blood, shed for you," the deacon said, as he held up the large, gold-colored goblet for me to drink out of. I looked down into the burgundy liquid, lowered my head, and took a sip. The wine was layered with flavors that lingered on my tongue and warmed my throat. This was my first experience of Communion wine. I felt vaguely naughty afterward; I had only ever had grape juice for Communion in church. Now I wondered why. Does wine have a story to tell about God that I don't know?

I was reared in a conservative Christian community without a positive view or theology of wine. In that absence, our thoughts on wine were shaped more by our theological priorities in order to avoid slippery slopes into sin and to look and live differently from "the world" outside our community. For us, that meant imposing safety zones of abstinence around behaviors or substances that seemed to have potential to draw us into the realm of temptation, sin, or, even worse, addiction.

There is wisdom in the desire to live faithfully as God's people, but ever since that Communion experience, I have explored a more biblical theology of wine. I recognize that such preemptive abstinence was unnecessary at best and spiritually harmful at worst. Ironically, my theological exploration of wine began at a Christian retreat, where I bought a book called *The Spirituality of Wine* as a gift for my wine aficionado uncle. Somehow that book never made it into my uncle's hands but still holds pride of place on my coffee table today. I have since discovered, like Pope Pius XII, that "wine in itself is an excellent thing."[1]

Eight thousand years ago, just outside the present-day city of Tbilisi (in modern-day Georgia), a small Stone Age village cultivated grapevines, crafted wine, and decorated jugs with grapes. The Gadachrili Gora community, along with their neighbors, are the world's earliest known vintners, precipitating an agricultural occupation that generations since have developed into an honored and sometimes holy vocation.[2] Celebration of wine and tales of its making have only ripened with time. To this day, wine retains a virtually universal appeal to humanity, transcending cultural, societal, geographical, linguistic, and temporal divides

People love wine and associate it with good things. Its portrayal in art, literature, and other cultural settings through the ages consistently signals joy, abundance, prosperity, feasting, hospitality, healing, remembrance, and enhanced connection between people and with deities. The Bible reflects a similar, overwhelmingly positive view of wine as a gift of God, emblematic of the exceptional abundance and feasting that will mark the final deliverance and restoration of God's people at the end of days.[3] God is described as a winemaker, as is Jesus (Matthew 21:33–43; Mark 12:1), who is altogether the vintner, the true vine (John 15:1–15), and the fruit of the vine that is crushed to produce the ultimate, most sublime wine of deliverance, justice, and communion (Revelation 14:19–20; 19:14–16).

As Christianity developed over generations, tradition affirmed the view that wine is a gift from God. Enjoyed in healthful moderation, it is life-giving and supports spiritual transformation. Most Christians through the ages into today continue to insist, like the early church father Cyprian, that wine is essential for celebrating the Eucharist, since Jesus himself established the sacrament using wine and because only wine can demonstrate the heart of the gospel sufficiently (*Epistle* 62).[4] Wow! The latter part of Cyprian's argument floored me when I first heard it. So, what gospel story does wine tell?

Hospitality, Gift, and Celebration

"Raise your glasses!" People use wine to show hospitality and honor, to mark rites of passage, and to make feasts and celebrations extra special. Clifton Fadiman, an American writer, once said in his book *Any Number Can Play*, "A bottle of wine begs to be shared; I have never met a miserly wine lover."[5] Biblical authors uniformly teach that hospitality toward strangers and the needy is the mark of people who love and reflect God's own hospitable character.[6] The early church practiced this virtue evangelistically every day, sharing their possessions with those in need and praising God and celebrating joyfully together with daily meals. Neighbors saw that Christians and their God welcomed and honored strangers and outcasts. In her instructive book *The Spirituality of Wine*, Gisela H. Kreglinger says there is much archaeological evidence that "wine, bread, and olive oil were the three main food groups of the Ancient Near Eastern and Mediterranean world," and wine was a common and likely daily drink for most families in and out of the Jewish culture.[7] The context of the Old and New Testaments spanned many years and across varied geography, but in all of those places and times wine was part of hospitality.

Jesus likened the kingdom of God to an extravagant banquet where undistinguished strangers would be welcomed and given places of honor (Matthew 22:8–10). Those who eat at God's feast are truly blessed. In this parable, Jesus was echoing Isaiah 25:6, where the prophet proclaims that Yahweh "will prepare a feast of rich food for all peoples, a banquet of aged wine—the best of meats and the finest of wines." Revelation also alludes to this in its mention of the "wedding feast of the Lamb" (Revelation 19:9 NLT). According to Revelation 19, Israel—now expanded to include people from every "tribe, nation, and tongue"—will be like a sparkling bride, wholly renewed, transformed, and perfected. And when she is finally united with her self-sacrificing, saving, and loving groom Jesus, then the party begins!

The Beauty and Hope of Community

Weddings are about celebrating the beginning of a special kind of intimacy and promise between a couple, but the ceremony also celebrates wider communal love. Loving communities birth individuals with the capacity to reproduce love. Love of God and people was at the root of all the laws that shaped the community of Israel and continues to shape the ethical priorities of Christian communities today. God's kind of love is hospitable and generous, so it is not surprising that the gospel of John portrays Jesus doing the first miracle of his ministry at a wedding, where love, hospitality, and generosity are in full swing.

God's kind of love is hospitable and generous.

When the host of this wedding unknowingly runs out of wine, Mary, Jesus's mother, clues him in to the shortage. Without making the groom look bad, Jesus solves the problem. He directs the stewards to fill six huge ceremonial washing jars with water before asking them to draw some out and take it to the party coordinator for approval (John 2:6). Upon sampling the wine, this man remarks to the groom that he has saved the best wine for now, which was against the typical custom of serving the best wine first. John ends the narrative abruptly, telling us that this was the beginning of the signs that Jesus performed that revealed his glory, and that his disciples believed in him (2:11).

In this miracle, Jesus prophetically rehearses his identity as the host of Yahweh's banquet and as the groom at the cosmic wedding to come.

The miracle itself and Jesus's use of the washing vessels draws my mind to four biblical passages that demonstrate this identity. First, way back in Exodus Yahweh demonstrates his total power over life, death, and creation when he turns all the water in Egypt, even within jugs, into blood (7:14–25). Here Jesus connects himself with Yahweh. Next, in Genesis 49:11 Jacob prophesies that someday Judah will tie up his donkey and colt to the choice vine and wash his clothing in the wine, commonly known as the blood of grapes. Messianic prophesies anticipate a savior from the line of Judah, as Jesus is, and foretell of the savior riding in victoriously on the foal of a donkey (Zechariah 9:9). This imagery of washing garments in wine is evoked and explained theologically in Revelation (7:14; 22:14), where the Messiah's followers effectively bleach their clothes by way of the Lamb's blood. God cleanses, purifies, and makes holy those who are faithful to the gospel to the very end. At Cana, Jesus foreshadows his impending sacrificial bloodshed that becomes the wine of salvation. He is making a statement that the cleansing and joyous feasting he provides will be superior in quantity and quality, overflowing in abundance!

With a glass-half-full theology we can enjoy the wine Jesus makes. We can be free to enjoy meals and celebrations with one another as Jesus did with so many. We can express hospitality by offering the wine of a great wedding feast to guests. We can especially celebrate the wine Jesus makes when we take the Eucharist and prayerfully receive it as a blessing, a symbol of the gospel, and a sign of the wedding feast of the Lamb to come. Jesus makes the *best* bubbly, and he doesn't skimp!

---

1. What is your experience with wine? Does your faith community have specific beliefs or traditions around wine?
2. How have you understood the scene of Jesus's miracle turning water into wine in Cana? Which other characters feel important to you (his mother Mary, the bride and groom, the host,

the servants, the guests)? Do you see yourself reflected in any of these characters?

3. What might it look like for your community to practice "abundance" and "joyous feasting"? What would an event look like that celebrated these? Who would attend?

Explore: Go to a local wine store. Do a tasting and find a wine you enjoy. Share the wine and a meal with friends.

Chapter 10

Jesus Was a Winemaker, Part Two

AMANDA WEBER

I am the true vine, and my Father is the gardener . . .
I am the vine, you are the branches.
—JOHN 15:1, 5

Have you ever held up a glass of wine, swirled it, and looked at the colors and movement? There is some beauty there. Even more, there is an essence of human history. Wine tells the beginning of our story, and the beginning of wine is the vine. To understand the biblical significance of Jesus's connection to the vine, it is necessary to look at the bookends of the Bible, starting with our humanity. In the beginning of our story, God places people in a garden and gives them a purpose: to live as his representatives in the world and be fruitful, multiply, and fill the earth. It is worth noting that ancient Near Eastern conceptions of creation focused on separating and enabling function and order from that which was previously stagnant, nonfunctional, and disordered. In other words, the invention of matter and materials is *not* what ancient people considered when talking about creation. What they really cared about was assigning order and purpose.

When the Bible was written, the cultivation of vineyards was viewed by ancients as a unique expression of bringing "order," a highly valued creation virtue and evidence of civility. This is important for two reasons. First, some ancient sources theorized that Eden was a vineyard and that the Tree of the Knowledge of Good and Evil in Eden was most likely understood by contemporaries to be a grapevine bearing grapes.[1] Flourishing vineyards were cross-culturally thought to be indicators of the blessing of the gods. This may explain why Noah planted a vineyard after the flood (Genesis 9:20). God makes a covenant with Noah and charges him, like Adam and Eve, to "be fruitful and multiply." Having just witnessed the unraveling of creation, Noah was probably eager to fulfill his charge and his calling. He plants and tends the vineyard and makes wine from its produce. But like Adam, his shame and nakedness are revealed when he "falls" into a drunken stupor (verses 20–21).

Looking Forward to Enjoying the Harvest

Similar to Noah, generation after generation of God's people enact echoes of the same story of faithfulness and failing. People are meant to live as representatives of God, continuing to uphold his kingdom and join in his ordering and filling work. They are meant to flourish, and their work in the land should also flourish. But God's people are unfaithful and sow destruction repeatedly. They cannot live up to their created identity. Natural consequences follow, and they become entrapped by the very destruction they planted. They return to disorder as they are exiled and scattered across the earth instead of gathered and constituted together. They work hard but may no longer enjoy the fruit of their labors. They may even reap a harvest, but it is turned over to their captors (Micah 6:15).

But in God's kingdom, all will be productive *and* enjoy the fruits of their work (Amos 9:13–15). This is how God created us to function: to be fruitful and flourish. When we don't, we are essentially becoming deformed. Messianic prophecies assure us that in the new age, we will be productive, our land will be fruitful, and we will be able to enjoy the fruit. These prophecies paint an expectation that the Messiah will provide the kind of rescue and salvation that will finally enable God's people to live out their God-given vocations as his fruitful and flourishing representatives.

Against this backdrop, Jesus says to his disciples, "I am the true vine, and my Father is the gardener [vine grower]. . . . I am the vine, you are the branches. If you remain in me and I in you, you will bear much fruit; apart from me you can do nothing" (John 15:1, 5). In these words, Jesus asserts his identity as God's Messiah by alluding to the vineyard language of the Old Testament prophets. He goes on to explain that the way to remain connected to him is to love one another in the self-giving style demonstrated by Jesus himself. The organizing principle of God's vineyard is generous love. Since vineyards are cultivated for wine, we can safely presume that the wine Jesus crafts from God's vineyard will be filled with all the complex notes that such love fosters.

Wine, Redemption, and Reversal

Wine reflects the trajectory—redemption and reversal—of our story within God's bigger story. While visions of Jesus as the vine, the messianic winemaker at the wedding in Cana, and the host of the feast in the new heavens and new earth summon up images of salvation, abundance, healing, festivals, and delight, Gisela Kreglinger reminds us that "the joy that comes from wine is a joy that's gone through the wine press."[2] In both the Old and New Testaments, we find images of God or his agents powerfully "treading the winepress" or delivering promised judgment to "sin-sick souls." Some of the language is gruesome, depicting God crushing his enemies like grapes. There are various traditions and methods of interpreting God's wrath and judgment in Scripture. The subject is important and emotional for most people and is worth studying in depth. But for now, I want to focus on what I think is an essential ingredient in any interpretive recipe. Like Jesus, Scripture is incarnational. God used human authors, who used the language and metaphors of their contexts to communicate the heart of God's message to his people. Scriptures that depict God's winepress-like judgment highlight God's just character and fierce protective love for his people. Sometimes they need to hear that God will defend them and bring justice, stop evil, and right wrongs. Other times, God's people turn away from God and behave as agents of injustice and evil in the world, and God remains just and merciful. He sends messengers and prophets to warn them, and he offers paths of redemption every time. Biblical salvation travels the same road as justice; healing cannot occur without ridding affliction from the scene. The two concepts are inseparable and messy. That they can be held together in true and complete goodness is mysterious to us and must only be possible through God's righteousness and wisdom. Whatever judgment will look like in the final days, the effect will be restoration, gathering, healing, and flourishing. Again, these texts were written primarily as hope-building, motivating prophecies to God's people, and redemption is always available to them.

Isaiah 53 depicts the suffering servant who was "pierced for our transgressions," as well as being "crushed for our iniquities," such that "the punishment that brought us peace was on him, and by his wounds we are healed" (verse 5). Christians traditionally have understood this passage as prophesying the iconoclastic aspect of Jesus as Messiah. He is victorious and powerful to save, but he does so by way of sacrificial love. In Isaiah 63, a figure in red-stained garments has "trodden the winepress alone" (verse 3); this has often been interpreted as Jesus engaging death directly by the power of his blood and achieving reversal for all who receive it!

The ancient Israelites and their pagan neighbors knew that "the life of every creature is its blood" (Leviticus 17:14), and wine was sometimes considered the blood of the gods.[3] "The annual harvest and crush of grapes was thought of as a ritual which reenacted that sacred moment of creation."[4] Winemaking requires regular cycles of life, death, and rebirth. Vines require periods of dormancy and pruning to thrive in warm weather. The grapes themselves must be crushed for the microbes to spread through the juice and transform the liquid. Through the winepress of justice, Jesus rescues and re-creates us. This is why celebrating the Last Supper, also known as Communion or the Eucharist, is such a joyful practice for Christians, and why using actual wine remains so important to many, especially of the contemplative persuasion.

Through the winepress of justice, Jesus rescues and re-creates us.

The Last Supper took place during the Passover season, one of the many times Jews incorporated wine into their remembrance celebrations. Passover recounts how God saved the Israelites by rescuing them from Egypt's oppression and enslavement. Passover also commemorates *how* God saved the Israelites by demonstrating his power over creation, alternate powers, and objects of worship. According to Exodus 12, before the final plague God instructed the Israelites to daub blood from a sacrificial lamb above their doorpost. For those who marked their doorposts accordingly, God would spare the lives of their firstborn sons. But those who chose not to would receive ultimate judgment in the death of their firstborn son. Metaphorically speaking, the plague of the firstborn reveals that God snuffs out the legacy of those who rival God's sovereignty and destroy his good kingdom. But Jesus says, "Those who eat my flesh and drink my blood abide in me and I in them" (John 6:56 NRSVUE), and "This is my blood of the covenant, which is poured out for many" (Mark 14:24 NRSVUE). Jesus is the vine, the fruit, the divine wine. Jesus makes all this from his body and love, and he serves it to the world as a remedy to restore all that has been desecrated in and around us. Jesus is the true vine, and a master winemaker!

Wine and the Holy Spirit

"Stop—you have to let it breathe first," my husband warned one evening as I embarked on "research" for these two essays. I was a skeptical newbie to enjoying wine and nearly missed out on experiencing that vintage at its best. I now know that wine is alive. Its making and enjoyment are a dynamic process that requires ceremony. This is not due to aesthetic preference or for spiritual priorities alone, but because of the molecular processes that occur all along the way. Rich, crumbly soil teams with life, and so does the summer breeze and powdery plump grape skins. All this life contributes to natural fermentation, along with any additional cultures or natural substances the winemaker blends in. Fermentation times vary dramatically depending on the type of wine and seasonal conditions. Some types continue to "ripen" even after bottling. Most wines, but especially complex varieties, reach their fullest potential only after adequate exposure to oxygen. This is normally achieved by simply pouring wine into decanters before serving and can take anywhere from minutes to hours. Vintners know that rushing through or prolonging any part of the process can destroy the life of the wine and spoil it. Jesus already decanted his most delightful, loving vintage; now the Holy Spirit is perfecting it.

I find this meditation instructive and hopeful when the stress and disappointments of this world overwhelm my anticipation for the great feast at Jesus's return. The underbelly of God's people seems to fill the frame from my point of view today. Jesus's life was already crushed and poured out for us. So where is the triumph? Where is the growth? Where is the glory? It is tempting to feel that the wine he made then is gone, dried up, or rancid. We often cannot see all that the Holy Spirit is doing to ferment and expand life in and around us. But perhaps it is simply resting in a decanter on the banquet table. When the time is right, we will pour the wine, raise our glasses together, breathe in, swirl, and drink in delight.

---

1. What geographic features in your community inspire you to see beauty in order? In what ways does your community benefit from this order? Have you seen "order" misapplied or become destructive?
2. Who do you know that models "remaining" in Jesus and being a "branch" attached to his "vine"? What does that look like specifically?
3. Who in your community needs to hear that "God will defend them and bring justice, stop evil, and right wrongs"? Have you experienced God's justice in your own life? What sustains you when justice seems far off?

Explore: Take a tour of a winery and reflect on the organization of the grounds and the growth of the grapevines. Try to grow a plant (any plant, it doesn't have to be a grapevine) and reflect on the different aspects of flourishing.

Chapter 11

Jesus Was Recentering the Commandments

SCOTT JOHANNINGSMEIER

> *Hear, O Israel: The* Lord *our God, the* Lord *is one. Love the* Lord *your God with all your heart and with all your soul and with all your strength. These commandments that I give you today are to be on your hearts.*
>
> —Deuteronomy 6:4–6

I remember when my oldest daughter entered kindergarten. She was so excited and nervous. Everything was new, and she wanted to do the right things and not mess up. So I found it funny when she came home with the school policy handbook and wanted me to read it to her. I tried to talk her out of it. "This will be boring, and you don't need to know everything in the handbook." Yet she insisted.

It wasn't long into the reading when she did get bored. However, she really wanted to know what to do at school, so she tried to push through. I could tell she was struggling with understanding every rule and policy in the handbook, so I closed it and set it on the table. She looked at me with a worried look, which revealed her fear of messing up at school. So I did what a father does. I told her, "There are really only two rules you need to follow. The first is to listen to your teacher and do what she asks you to do. The second rule is to be nice to the other kids. If you do these two, then you will be fine and you will not break any of the school rules."

Following the Commandments: A Juggling Act

The intimidation my daughter felt at hearing the school rules is something we all feel, especially when it comes to obeying the commandments. There are a lot of commandments in the Bible. Have you read them? Even if you tried, you would find yourself getting bored and confused. My daughter's teacher understood the rules and could give her instructions to follow. The religious teachers of Jesus's day knew the commandments and likewise gave instructions on how to follow them. But even that became confusing.

As the religious leaders worked to help people understand and follow the commandments, they eventually had a system with 613 laws. They came to this number because they found 613 laws in the Pentateuch, the first five books in the Bible, and there are 613 letters, in Hebrew, in the text of the Ten Commandments. The religious leaders were able to divide the commandments into subgroups. There were 365 "do not" passages, one for each day, and 248 "do" passages, one for each part of the human body based upon their understanding of anatomy. Within the subgroups, they even divided the commands into binding and nonbinding commands.[1]

Is there any wonder why there were questions about the commandments? The religious leaders of Jesus's day—the Pharisees, Sadducees, and teachers of the law—were trying to help the people understand and obey the commandments. They wanted to faithfully follow God's commands and not mess up, just as the religious leaders of our day also attempt to help us understand how to live in God's will. Therefore, there was a lot of debate about the nature and "weight" of the commandments. All the commandments were considered sacred as they were delivered by Moses. However, there was some debate among the rabbis about which commandments were more important.[2]

The Greatest Commandment

These debates about the importance of the commandments serve as the background to the story we know as the Greatest Commandment found in Matthew 22, Mark 12, and Luke 10. While the story occurs in three different gospels, it is told slightly different in each one to emphasize a theme of that gospel. In Matthew and Luke, the question the religious leaders ask Jesus is meant to test him in order to catch him up in his words. Mark, however, uses a different tone for the question.

In Mark 12 the religious leaders grill Jesus on social issues, such as paying taxes to Caesar, as well as theological issues, like what marriage looks like after the resurrection. During this grill session,

> one of the teachers of the law came and heard them debating. Noticing that Jesus had given them a good answer, he asked him, "Of all the commandments, which is the most important?" (verse 28)

There is no deception in the question as recorded in Mark. It comes from a place of devotion and seeking answers.

Where would you start to find an answer to his question? For Jesus the answer was clear.

> "The most important one," answered Jesus, "is this: 'Hear, O Israel: The Lord our God, the Lord is one. Love the Lord your God with all your heart and with all your soul and with all your mind and with all your strength.'" (verses 29–30)

The Old Testament passage from which Jesus quotes has long been at the very heart of Jewish religious life. It is found in Deuteronomy

6 and is known as the *Shema*, which means "hear" in Hebrew. The Shema was already a prominent component of prayer and worship within the Jewish practices of Jesus's day. Through this passage the Jewish people learn there is one God and only one God. They are to love the one true God with their heart, soul, and strength.

In many ways, Jesus's answer to the question is a pretty safe option. Since the Shema was such an integral part of Jewish life, it would be difficult to find a more important command. However, what Jesus does next is not the safe option. He proceeds to add to the Shema another command, this one found in Leviticus 19:18. Imagine school-aged children in the United States coming home and saying they learned a new version of the Pledge of Allegiance. How much uproar would that cause? So, when Jesus adds to such an important text as the Shema, we should take note.[3]

> The second [most important command] is this: "Love your neighbor as yourself." There is no commandment greater than these. (Mark 12:31)

What a revolutionary twist. The teacher of the law asks which commandment (singular) is the most important and where he should focus his attention, and Jesus gives him two to live by. Loving others is a central part of the Jewish faith. There are numerous passages that champion the care of the orphaned, widowed, and foreigner.[4] Yet caring for the needy is not part of the Shema. Most teachers or rabbis would have responded to Jesus by saying the former is greater than the latter.

Jesus has restructured the commandments for this teacher. Following the law is no longer about doing what is right or not doing what is wrong. Understanding the commandments is about how and who we love. Love God and love others is the answer Jesus gives as a new cohesive commandment. In Matthew's account, Jesus finishes by saying, "All the Law and the Prophets hang on these two commandments"

(22:40). This rocks the world of this teacher, and he realizes he will need to recenter everything he thought he knew.[5]

The teacher of the law asks which commandment is the most important, and Jesus gives him two to live by.

Mark's account ends with the words: "And from then on no one dared ask him any more questions" (12:34). When we focus on Jesus's call to love God and love others, the question "Which commandment is the greatest?" becomes irrelevant. With his groundbreaking answer, Jesus changed the entire focus of their debate. Jesus told them what is the greatest, and it is to love. When you focus on loving God *and* loving others, you cannot be wrong.

My daughter is now a freshman in high school, and the same two rules about how to behave in school still apply: Listen to what your teacher says, and be nice to the other students. Yet we know that high school is not as easy as kindergarten. There is a lot going on as you try to figure out who you are and how you relate to others around you. While there are many people ready to give advice on how to live, I believe Jesus showed us how to take all the noise of life and filter it through a simplified lens. In everything we do and all the situations we face, the questions we should ask ourselves are, "Am I loving God with everything I am?" and "Am I showing love to others in the ways I want to be loved?" There are no greater commandments than these.

---

1. How do your body and emotions respond to handbooks or rule books? Do you have the same response when reading through all the different commandments in the first five books of the Bible?
2. In your faith community, which commandments are emphasized as being important?

3. Does loving God and loving others feel like a comprehensive explanation for how to live? Are there particular situations in your life where this feels either helpful or unhelpful?

Explore: Read a handbook for an organization or group that you participate in. Write out how you would summarize it in only a couple of sentences.

Chapter 12

Jesus Was Not Politically Powerful

AMANDA CLARK

My kingdom is not of this world.
—JOHN 18:36

I spent my childhood in a very small home filled to the brim with seven siblings. We had taken over every part of the house except for one small closet in my parents' room. The tiny closet was just big enough for a few mementos of my parents' youth in a messy, overstuffed filing cabinet. Because it represented the people they had been before we kids existed, I was fascinated with this collection and curiously picked through all of it. I picked up a Nixon bumper sticker, the paper backing still in place, with a picture of a peace symbol and the words "Footprint of an American Chicken" on it. Though I neither understood the symbol nor the message, the image burned into my mind.

In my adulthood I learned that my dad offered his teenage vigor to the Republican party. He attended a Nixon rally and even got to shake his hand, albeit with an overly enthusiastic two-handed pump that prompted the Secret Service guard walking alongside Nixon to tell Dad to back up. This is a perfect picture of my father: a wildly expressive man who sees the world in black and white and is 100 percent engaged in what he believes in.

Only a couple of years later, Dad's life was forever changed when he became involved in a revival movement that trickled down from the Jesus People of the 1970s. He experienced the power of the Holy Spirit, witnessed miracles of physical healing, and found a community of people who passionately worshipped Jesus and believed Christianity should involve total life transformation. This church eventually embraced a separatist mindset, choosing to withdraw from the wickedness of society. The result was that he left behind his bumper stickers and raised his children to eschew any Christian involvement in politics. He lectured us on the errors of the social justice gospel, believing that in its attempt to do the good works of Jesus through activism, it had sold out to the world and abandoned the true gospel of Jesus. To him, the life and ministry of Jesus was not in any way political. Jesus's power was different.

But is this true? Many people believe Jesus was deeply political, and even an influential political figure in his day. They see his death as an indicator of his high level of involvement and the threat he posed to Rome. Many Christians believe it is our duty to be involved in politics and vote according to Christian ethics. What makes it hard to assess whether or not Jesus was politically powerful is that, in the American experience, *politics* can be a loaded word. Simply uttering the word can evoke strong emotional responses. The word *politics* means the art or science of gaining influence and power in government. The mere survival of Christianity since the time of Jesus demonstrates that he was excellent in gaining influence. In word and deed Jesus was powerful, but was he trying to gain that influence and power in government? If so, was he successful in becoming politically powerful?

It's safe to say that many people in Jesus's day wanted him to be politically powerful. In Luke's gospel we read that before Jesus was even born, he was expected to be political and to change the social order (Luke 1:46–55). When Mary learned she was pregnant with the Messiah, Judea had been occupied by Rome for over sixty years. Rome maintained empirical control by crushing any form of rebellion, setting up shrines to the emperor, and taxing the Jewish people into a wealth gap that kept most of the population extremely poor. Even so, the faithful of Israel had been waiting so long for God to send them the Messiah, God's promised anointed king whom many believed would deliver them from Rome. Indeed, when God the Father at Jesus's baptism proclaimed, "You are my Son" (Luke 3:22 NRSVUE), those four words affirmed to Jesus his status as God's Messiah. In that moment, Jesus could well have decided it was his mission to restore the throne of Israel. Immediately following his baptism, Jesus had a tremendous opportunity to pursue political power, but he turned it down.

A Different Kind of Political Power

According to Luke 4, following his baptism, Jesus spent forty days in the desert, where he was presented with a juicy shortcut to political power by joining forces with Satan. Instead, Jesus rejected this temptation and walked out of the desert and back to Galilee filled with the power of the Holy Spirit and a resoluteness of purpose (verses 5–8). Jesus then gave his first message in the synagogue in Galilee, reading from Isaiah's prophecy of the coming Messiah who would bring good news to the poor and bring about the kind of Jubilee that Israel had never known, where debts would be forgiven and the lowest and least-resourced in society would be given new freedom and access to flourishing (verses 16–19). Jesus ended that sermon by saying it had been fulfilled (verse 21), meaning that he believed himself to be the one who would bring about the social change of which Isaiah spoke.

When Jesus spoke these words, it must have been electrifying, and he knew why. Many of the Jewish people during that time were waiting for a prophesied messiah who would overthrow Rome, take back the throne, and rule the nations.[1] But Jesus did not come to reestablish the kingdom of Israel; he came to establish the kingdom of God on earth. In that sense, Jesus was deeply political. He came to be King. He came to rule. But the kingdom he announced was not of this world, and it did not operate according to the political structure of this world. Jesus would not rule through political coercion or power, but he would accept his crown.

Jesus came to be King. He came to rule. But the kingdom he announced was not of this world.

Instead of gathering a rebel army or courting the favor of the religious elite, Jesus gathered male and female followers from both ends of the social hierarchy. He created an alternative community through demonstrations and messages like the Sermon on the Mount. In this community, instead of vying for power and position, Jesus's followers practiced radical commitment to morally distinct, godly community (Matthew 5:48) by loving their enemies (verse 44; Luke 6:27), eating with sinners (Mark 2:16; Luke 15:2), rejecting the accumulation of hoarded wealth (Matthew 6:19; Luke 12:15–21; 19:8–10), and taking care of the poor (Matthew 5:2–9; 19:21) and outcast (Luke 8:26–39). As Jesus gathered followers, he told them of the kingdom of God that was arriving in him and of the loyalty that would be required to accommodate this new regime. He made it clear that he knew his political agenda would challenge those in power and that following him would come at a cost (Matthew 16:24; Mark 13:9).

Jesus's ministry came under growing pressure as the religious leaders began to feel threatened by the authority with which Jesus taught and the incredible power he possessed to discern their thoughts, heal the sick, and raise the dead. Jesus openly opposed the Jewish religious leadership's social order in Jerusalem because it was so unlike the kingdom of God. In that sense, Jesus was political.

Jesus was also powerful. In the power of the Spirit, Jesus did miracles that demonstrated the arrival of a kingdom that gave preference to the lowly. He healed the sick and restored them to the community from which their illness often excluded them. He claimed to be sent from God, and even one with the Father, and he backed up such claims with convincing action. He boldly rode into Jerusalem on a donkey the week of his death (Matthew 21; Mark 11; Luke 19; John 12). Several clues indicate that this processional act was a sign to his followers that he was announcing his kingship. Matthew quotes Zechariah 9:9, that prophesies a king riding on a donkey. The gospel writers also observe how people spread their cloaks on the road before him, hearkening to 2 Kings 9:13 where cloaks are spread for a newly anointed king of Israel, and cry out "Hosanna" (meaning "save us" in Hebrew) to Jesus, the messianic "Son of David." In Jesus the kingdom of God came rushing upon the earth, and Jesus spent his ministry years gaining power and influence in this new government.

Not the Power of Rome or Israel

However, Jesus was not powerful in the politics of Rome or of Israel, and this disappointed many followers, including his disciples. Jesus's followers believed he was the Messiah, and they understood the Messiah to be a conquering warrior and king (Mark 10:35–40; Luke 22:49). Case in point, though Jesus predicts his death three times in Mark's gospel, the disciples never believe him because in their worldview, Jesus came to start a revolution and overthrow Rome (Acts 1:8). They did not hear Jesus when he repeatedly told them he had come to be a servant. Matthew's gospel makes it clear that at his arrest, Jesus had the command of a legion of angels (26:53). But Peter brandished his sword at Jesus's arrest, and Jesus shut him down (John 18:10).

Jesus knew neither Rome nor the Sanhedrin were the real enemy and that his true power would come in laying down his life. In Jesus's death and resurrection, he gained victory over sin and death and broke

Satan's grip on the world. He was successful in establishing the kingdom of God on earth, and *that* government now rests on his shoulders and will never end. Jesus was not politically powerful because he did not come to gain governmental power in our world systems; it was never part of his plan to overthrow Rome. Jesus was the Messiah, and he does reign victorious as King, but he would not be the Messiah his people wanted because his kingdom was not of this world (John 18:36).

When my father abandoned politics for Jesus, he did it because he found a community that, for a time, practiced the kind of alternative community Jesus was building. However, like holding on to his Nixon bumper sticker from 1968, I do not think he ever gave up an affinity for war or even political ideologies. At least that is what his love of Churchill biographies and a private renewal of interest in the Republican party tells me. It is difficult to give up firmly held concepts about how society works to maintain order and position in the world. Jesus was at every turn faced with this choice too—either to become politically powerful or to teach his followers a new way of being in the world. With gratitude I have placed my trust in Jesus's redeeming death and resurrection as part of this new way, rather than in the political power systems of this world.

---

1. In what ways is the name of "Jesus" used to gain political power? How do you interact with politically powerful people? What type of politicians does your local community elevate?
2. Have you ever been placed in a government position in your community? What could it look like for a Christian to hold an influential position in government?
3. What aspects of "firmly held concepts about how society works" and "how . . . to maintain order and position in the world" should your local community rethink? Could upending the way things are benefit your community? How would you participate in this?

Explore: Listen to a podcast exploring politics and religion, such as *The Holy Post* with Phil Vischer and Skye Jethani, or read Tim Keller's article "Reflections on Faith and Politics." Reflect on Jesus's choices in regard to political power and how you might model those same choices in your own life and community.

Chapter 13

Jesus Was Kind

ELIZABETH DAIGLE

But to you who are willing to listen, I say, love your enemies! Do good to those who hate you. Bless those who curse you. Pray for those who hurt you. If someone slaps you on one cheek, offer the other cheek also. If someone demands your coat, offer your shirt also. Give to anyone who asks; and when things are taken away from you, don't try to get them back. Do to others as you would like them to do to you.

—Luke 6:27–31 (NLT)

With the ache in his legs too strong to ignore, the man heaved a sigh and told his friends, "You go on ahead. I'll wait here." The center of town was empty in the heat of the day, but there was a small patch of shade near the well. He sat down on its wall, shoulders slumped, arms draped loosely in his lap. He closed his eyes and breathed slowly, working to disengage a tired body and mind, but he was beckoned back all too soon by the sound of approaching footsteps.

A woman walked toward him without seeing him, her eyes steady on the road. When Jesus heard her sigh, he remembered his own exhaustion, for the heat of the day spared no one. As she approached, he startled her with a question, "Will you get me something to drink?"

She was confused. Why was *he* asking *her*? During their short conversation she realized Jesus was more than a weary rabbi. He was a prophet who, in his rejection of her cautiously veiled answers, proved he cared enough about her to get to the heart of her story. He knew there was more behind her words and refused to let her stay in the gray of pretending. You see, Jesus was kind.

Kindness Beyond Niceness

Kind is different than polite. If Jesus had been content with polite with the woman at the well in John 4, willing to stay within social protocols, he would have moved from the wall of the well so she could draw water without hindrance or conversation. But Jesus was too kind to let her stay where she was. He pushed her, he challenged her, and he invited her to see the truth.

We often confuse kindness with niceness. But kindness is much more than holding doors for others, giving compliments, and sending smiley-face emojis. Kindness is complicated. In fact, real kindness can teeter on the uncomfortable. But like a lifeguard scanning the water, kindness can be the life preserver thrown to the flailing swimmer in the deep end of the pool, but only if they're willing to grab hold.

God uses kindness to pull us to safety. Romans 2:4 declares it is God's kindness that leads us to repentance. Kindness isn't glossing over a reality, pretending all is well when it isn't. Kindness is facing reality head-on. And in that way, kindness is linked to conviction. Ultimately, it is no kindness to withhold live-giving treatment to the dying because the procedure will produce momentary pain. So it is with God's kindness. The truth of our failures brings pain, the reality of what our sin will earn brings remorse. But as we face that pain and the stark reality of our need for Jesus, we have what we need to find life. We experience God's mercy because he draws us with kindness.

Kindness grows from an intentional awareness of others. It's not just observation; it's lovingly noticing others. And that quality of noticing births acts of kindness rooted in the choice to prioritize the needs of others. Jesus exemplified kindness. He sacrificially served while overlooking his own weariness or safety. He was kind to those who were hurting and to those who hurt him. He was kind to his friends and to his enemies, to the powerful and to the invisible.

Kindness grows from an intentional awareness of others.

When the lepers came, whom no one would look at, let alone touch, Jesus brought them healing by reaching out and laying his hands on them (Matthew 8:1–3). When a suffering woman reached for him in the crowd, and he felt the Father's healing power flow through him, he immediately stopped. As she cowered before him, fearful of rebuke, he called her "daughter," not content to bring healing only to her body—he also had to heal her heart (Mark 5:30–34). When four friends lowered their paralyzed companion down through the roof, Jesus wasn't satisfied with physical healing alone but pointed to the deeper need of healing from sin (Mark 2:1–12). He was too kind to let anyone stay in sin or suffering.

Kindness flows so easily from those who love well; it appears as effortless as water over smooth rocks. But like real love, kindness has a cost. In fact, it can cost quite a lot because it requires something of both parties. Those who offer it must be willing to shoulder its inconveniences and potential for misunderstanding, and those who receive it must be humble enough to keep their hands cupped so as not to drop it. There is sacrifice on both sides.

Jesus wasn't just kind to those who were earnest and seeking. What's remarkable is that Jesus was kind to *everyone*. He was kind to the unkind. He repaid evil with kindness (Luke 23:34). He extended healing to those who hated him. During his arrest in the garden of Gethsemane, hours before he was sentenced to die, an overzealous defender sliced off the ear of one of the men in the crowd (22:50–51). Yet even as the cloak of evil fell, Jesus fought back with kindness, completely restoring the man from his wound.

Jesus's kindness extended beyond his compassionate healing. He dismantled the stone walls of stereotypes. He ministered to the person in front of him, the blind one who called from the road, and the unsavory tax collector who waited for him up in the tree (Matthew 15:30–31; Luke 18:35–43; 19:1–7). It did not matter if they were poor or rich, right or wrong, Jew or Gentile. Jesus looked past circumstances, sickness, and station. He saw withered limbs and breathless bodies but, while attending to the urgent and obvious, he pushed into the chronic and deep.

Kindness Goes Deeper

In his kindness Jesus brought relief not just to the physical symptoms of disease and disability but also to the deeper needs housed within the heart of the hurting. Because Jesus wasn't satisfied with temporary. He cared about the suffering around him but always focused on the eternal.

According to John 11, when Jesus's friend Lazarus fell sick, his sisters Martha and Mary called for Jesus. Jesus didn't go to them at first and Lazarus died. When Jesus finally went to see them, he had a conversation with Martha on the road where she met him. Martha said, "If you had been here, my brother would not have died" (verse 21). Jesus didn't disagree or explain his delay but invited her into a deeper understanding of who he was. He told her if she believed, she would see the glory of God (verse 40). He declared that he was the resurrection and the life (verse 25). He used her disappointment with him, her questioning of his goodness, and her confusion regarding his kindness to convey the deeper truths about eternal life. Then he raised Lazarus from the dead.

Random acts of kindness are "in" these days. Whether we *do* them or not, we all like to *hear* about them. News stations often close their evening broadcasts with feel-good stories about kindness in real time. I've got to be honest. I know it's a ploy to keep me tuned in, but following a deluge of the downright disturbing, I'm happy to hold on for the predictable palate cleansing end as a way of reminding myself all is not lost. I can listen all day to the stories of lost dogs being found, communities rallying around their disabled neighbors, and nondescript heroes who show up with a casserole, a shovel, or a wad of cash when it matters. Kindness should win any election with a landslide. Everyone loves kindness. We admire it, even crave it, so why is it so hard to find? Why is there such a short supply?

Maybe it's because ideas are easy but the actions are hard. And maybe it's because in our kindness quest we've been looking in the wrong places. Perhaps we've been trying to muster up kindness out of the well of our own hearts, not aware there's a leak in the lining. Rather than promoting kindness with posters on Pinterest or mounting magnets on our fridge, we need to go to the source: Jesus. When we find him, we need to follow him and then draw from his well of living water and drink deeply.

I want that cold, cold water from deep in the depths of the well, where it's dark, peaceful, and pure. There is kindness there, and it will never run dry.

---

1. Have you recently heard a feel-good news story about kindness that deeply resonated with you? How did your body and emotions respond to this story? What moved you?
2. Describe a time when you had to choose between being kind and being polite. What social etiquette did you need to navigate? Were you accused of making the situation uncomfortable? What course of action did you choose? Would you choose that same action today?
3. Do the messages in your church link the trait of kindness with

deeper eternal truths? How can a faith community show kindness in broader society? What should your faith community do if their acts of kindness are misunderstood?

Explore: Reflect on how you see the eternal truths in stories of kindness. Would similar acts of kindness be interpreted as eternal truths in your community?

Chapter 14

Jesus Was Humble

MELISSA PILLMAN

> *The greatest among you must be a servant. But those who exalt themselves will be humbled, and those who humble themselves will be exalted.*
>
> —Matthew 23:11–12 (NLT)

We recently had a new pastor start on staff at our church. Upon meeting him and considering his character, I used the word *humble* as a positive attribute to describe him, as he appeared to be someone who would be willing to work on projects together, not someone always needing to grab the reins. He seemed postured to learn rather than someone who would come in assuming he had it all figured out already. I believe that he will readily share opportunities to develop others, even at his own expense, rather than hoard the limelight. In a word, he seems *humble*, and I look forward to partnering with him in ministry. Humility is generally a *good* thing, although not a terribly *costly* thing, in this context.

However, in the ancient Mediterranean world humility was not always viewed as a positive personal quality or as a virtue.[1] Indeed, the kind of humility that Jesus taught about would be considered demeaning and degrading to us today. To understand this, you have to put yourself in the shoes (or sandals) of a first-century Jew living in

Judea under Roman imperial rule. You are surrounded by a complex system where social, political, and religious structures are all intertwined. You are well versed in the unwritten rules that define status based on ethnicity, gender, social class, and family. You are also well acquainted with the dominant cultural currency of honor and shame, where the positive path led toward elevated honor and the feared path was marked with the humiliation of shame.

No one wanted to be humble. Except Jesus.

Honoring Humility

The people of God had been waiting for God's presence to return—a Messiah, the one promised through Scripture who would bring restoration to the people of Israel. When people began to hope that Jesus might just be that guy, their imagination (groomed by their culture) instantly settled on the idea that Jesus would emerge as a messianic king! Jesus would overthrow Roman rule and bring restoration and victory to the people of God once again, people who had been humbled far too long. Even when Jesus repeatedly told his followers that his path would be hard, that he would be betrayed to his enemies, and that he would even face death, they still turned and started immediately arguing about who among them would be the greatest (Luke 9:44–48). If I were in Jesus's place, I imagine I would have been shaking my head and burying my face in my hands. But I find hope in this: While teaching "whoever is the least among you is the greatest" (verse 48 NLT), Jesus held a child.

What?! Where's the victory and conquest in that? It's understandable that Jesus would teach that honor should not be based on power or position, especially over against others (as was the nature of the honor-shame cultural currency of the Roman world), but can't honor be bestowed based on deeper virtues?[2] Not for Jesus. For him, honor goes to those who willingly humble themselves (14:10–11). Yes, in some extreme cases, that may mean being willing to lay down one's life for someone else (John 15:13). But more often, it means the hundreds of little, everyday ways that we can "lay ourselves down" for the good of someone else. In a sense, humility can be interpreted as serving others[3] and honoring them as someone who matters. We set aside our desire to be praised and instead pass the credit to those who helped behind the scenes. We set aside our right to get even and instead seek to help the one who is hurting. We stop grasping for advancement so that it can be handed to someone who might otherwise be overlooked.

For Jesus, honor goes to those who willingly humble themselves.

Jesus demonstrated this humility most shockingly on his willing walk to the cross, disregarding the shame (Hebrews 12:2) for the joy and victory that his path accomplished for others. The humility of the cross becomes the shape of divine love—the fullness of God (Father, Son, and Spirit) taking on the muck and yuck of human sin upon the shoulders of the one who deserved none of it (the Son of God). At the crucifixion, the fullness of God was executed in a way saved for the worst criminals and people of low standing (no Roman citizens were crucified, as it was too shameful). The shame of the cross was the ultimate act of humility, and Jesus took what the world saw as shameful and turned it into something beautiful. The resurrection became the ultimate victory. God in Jesus defeated all that darkness and evil had in their arsenal, and then he spent that victory on us—he shared it as a free gift. And now, standing in that victory, we lay down our lives for others. Sounds like a strange reversal, but such is the way of Jesus.

Living as Humble Followers

But why? Why does the path of following Jesus prioritize humility? Romans 12:3 reminds us not to think of ourselves more highly than we should, remembering that we all need one another. Yes, I think there is value in avoiding pride, but the call to humility goes beyond that. It's a life of spending outward. When you stand secure in how very loved you are by God, you can spend that love outward because it overflows without measure. When you stand free of sin because you've been forgiven through grace, you can spend that grace outward because you no longer feel like it's your job to judge others. When you stand in the overflow of Jesus's self-giving sacrifice, you can spend that sacrifice toward someone else in need—even if it comes at a cost to you.

Okay so far, right? Don't think you're a big deal (avoid pride) and be thoughtful toward others (be kind). Sounds like a checklist to be a nice person, so Jesus must be teaching "ways to be good so we can get into heaven." Allow me to step onto a soap box for just a moment. Far too many Christians have thought that their salvation was for some future date: a get-into-heaven-free card. So they assume that Jesus's teaching about things like humility is designed to help us be good in the meantime while we hold on to that card for the pearly gates moment. But Jesus offers so much more—he offers freedom, salvation, and a God-designed way for living *in the here and now* that involves loving God (in right relationship with God) and loving others (because we're hardwired for healthy relationships). If you live that way and others do as well, suddenly we taste a bit of heaven here and now. There's no room for hierarchies, power abuse, racism, sexism, or any other "-ism" that elevates *self* over *another*. We emulate the servant-postured, self-spending humility of Christ (read Philippians 2:3–11).

Jesus teaches that "God blesses those who are humble, for they will inherit the whole earth" (Matthew 5:5 NLT). That can be deceiving to our ears, sounding like a spiritual barter that if we are humble, we'll be blessed and get lots of land (i.e., prosperity). These words come at the start of Jesus's Sermon on the Mount, in which he takes the cultural value system of the day and turns it upside down. God is doing something altogether new, and those who live in the way of this kingdom will find fulfillment of the promises of old. Jesus refers to the promise given to the people of God to inherit a land where they would be able to live in peace and holiness with God.[4] And while we wait for a future heaven, Jesus shows us a way to live into that future right where we are today. We live humbly not because we want the reward of prosperity, but because we follow a humble Christ. We are safe to receive his love and grace without a hoarding mentality, because he has given it so lavishly that we can *spend ourselves* for the benefit of others. Because, at the end of the day, the fountain of love and grace will not run dry. We humbly spend from the overflow of what's been lavishly poured out to us.

---

1. When have you felt most enabled to love other people? Are there spiritual practices that help empower you to live in this way?
2. How do you sense the Holy Spirit's direction in living humbly? Do you "taste a bit of heaven here and now" in these situations?
3. Of everyone you know, who best models Jesus's humility?

Explore: Commit for a couple of weeks or even a month to praying and asking God to help you better understand the depth and breadth of God's love for you so that you can lavish it on other people. Reflect on how your attitude and actions toward other people transform over the month.

Chapter 15

Jesus Was Merciful

ANNE MACKIE MORELLI

Let us therefore approach the throne of grace with boldness, so that we may receive mercy and find grace to help in time of need.
—HEBREWS 4:16 (NRSVUE)

Several years ago, our family walked through a series of major losses and trials. Of all the ordeals we faced, I personally found the hardest to navigate was walking alongside our three adult sons as they wrestled with their own challenges and heartaches. As their mother, I was devastated when one of our sons experienced a broken heart, another experienced a searching heart, and a third experienced a grieving heart. However, as so often happens, even in the darkest circumstances, rays of light broke through.

Throughout that grinding season of adversity, I watched as our sons rallied, cared for each other, and trusted in God's daily provision and mercy. I witnessed how others from our community stepped up to provide empathetic and practical support. Our sons' courage, tenacity, and faith, combined with such tender acts of mercy, contributed to their healing and a reshaping of their individual and our collective stories. Even though this season of sorrow is now relegated to a chapter in our family's narrative, abundant mercy will always remain an overarching theme.

Every single one of us will face adversity and suffering in our lifetime. Trials of some kind or another are eventually woven into every human narrative. Yet even when we're able to cognitively acknowledge this truth, we will go to almost any length to avoid hardship. Typical grief avoidance strategies include behaviors such as distancing ourselves from suffering, dissociating from the reality of our circumstances, putting a positive spin on events, suppressing our pain and discomfort, holding grudges, engaging in denial, chasing distractions, or using substances to numb the pain. But Jesus shows us a better way. He encourages us to lean into suffering, to process loss and grief, and to turn to him and trust in his abundant mercy, compassion, and love.[1]

Mercy is a facet of God's love. It is akin to other components of God's love such as compassion, gentleness, goodness, kindness, and forgiveness. God's mercy manifests itself in both his immeasurable empathy for those who suffer *and* his acting to relieve their burdens. God's heart aches when we are in pain; he yearns to respond to our afflictions. In his mercy, God leans into our distress and seeks to facilitate our healing and restoration. Such mercy is astounding because it even extends to those who may appear undeserving and to those who are unable to provide for themselves.

Due to our human nature, some of our suffering is caused by our own poor decisions and sinful behavior. This happens whenever our errant behavior generates discord and misery for ourselves and for others. Typically, this suffering is perceived as being a logical or a deserved consequence of our unhealthy choices. On the other hand, we also experience adversity that is random and inexplicable, or that has been caused by someone else's immoral behavior. This type of adversity is generally referred to as being undeserved or unfair. Narratives highlighting both deserved and undeserved human suffering echo throughout Scripture and illuminate how God's merciful heart intersects with our human suffering.

Jesus Offers Mercy

One such narrative occurs in Mark 5, when we are introduced to a woman who had been hemorrhaging for twelve years. She had been unable to find relief from her physical ailment and emotional anguish despite consulting with numerous physicians. In addition, her torment had been further complicated by several factors. She had endured the physicians' various treatments and had spent all her money on trying to find relief. Yet her health had only deteriorated. Furthermore, according to the religious laws of the time, she had been declared unclean and cast out of her community, because the law stated that if anyone were to touch her or anything that she had touched, they too would become unclean (Leviticus 15:19–33). As a result, she had been socially isolated and shamed for twelve years. Extensive physical, emotional, social, financial, and spiritual suffering had become woven into her narrative.[2]

In his mercy, God leans into our distress and seeks to facilitate our healing and restoration.

But when she heard about Jesus, she had faith he could heal her and turned to him for help. As this unclean woman audaciously pressed through the crowd toward Jesus, she thought to herself, "If I but touch his cloak, I will be made well" (Mark 5:28 NRSVUE). The moment she reached out and touched it, her hemorrhaging ceased and she was healed. Jesus immediately felt power leave his body as the woman grabbed his cloak. He stopped, turned around, and asked who had touched him. His disciples dismissed his inquiry and suggested it was just the people in the crowd pressing in around him. But Jesus persisted. He continued to scan the crowd, and even though there was an urgency to minister to a young girl who was dying, Jesus was determined to connect with whoever had touched him. The woman decided to tell Jesus the truth. His response to the woman was merciful. He tenderly replied, "Daughter, your faith has made you well; go in peace, and be healed of your disease" (Mark 5:34 NRSVue).

The narrative of the hemorrhaging woman elucidates how when we have faith, and trust Jesus with our suffering, he will welcome us with open arms, a heart full of compassion, and overflowing mercy—even if we are the outcast, poor, vulnerable, sick, shamed, weary, unloved, broken, or bruised.

Our Response to Mercy

In his book *Knowing God*, J. I. Packer declares, "The measure of love is how much it gives, and the measure of the love of God is the gift of his only Son to become human and to die for our sins, and so become the one mediator who can bring us to God."[3] So how might we respond to God's divine love and lavish mercy?

We can find the answers throughout Scripture. John wrote, "Beloved, let us love one another, because love is from God; everyone who loves is born of God and knows God. Whoever does not love does not know God, for God is love" (1 John 4:7–8 NRSVue). Thus, because God is love, and love flows from God, we can rest in the assurance that out of his extravagant love flows extravagant mercy. In his gospel account Luke writes, "Be merciful, just as your Father is merciful" (6:36 NRSVue). And Jesus goes one step further when he beseeches us not only to love those we deem as being worthy of our love or who will love us back, but also to love and be merciful toward all others in all circumstances (Mark 12:30–31). Finally, the Bible also provides practical examples of how we should demonstrate such love and mercy, which includes feeding the hungry, giving water to the thirsty, clothing the naked, sheltering the homeless, caring for the sick, and visiting the imprisoned (Matthew 25:31–40) as well as acting justly and remaining humble (Micah 6:8; Luke 6:36–37) along with being tolerant and forgiving someone even when you have a grievance against them (Matthew 18:22).

Yet in our humanity we can find it difficult to extend such generous love and mercy toward others consistently, especially when they have caused our suffering. However, one of the most profound outcomes of receiving God's mercy, as evidenced throughout Scripture, is that his love and mercy have the power to soften and shape hearts. Over time as the recipients of his mercy, our hearts are transformed and we become more compassionate and emulate Jesus's lavish mercy, even toward those who have wounded us.

As humans it can be hard for us to grasp the full scope of divine mercy. Yet its breadth and depth pulses throughout Scripture and is visible through accounts like that of the hemorrhaging woman. Jesus promises, "Listen! I am standing at the door, knocking; if you hear my voice and open the door, I will come in and eat with you, and you with me" (Revelation 3:20 NRSVUE).

Jesus the merciful awaits. All we must do in response is seek him, have faith, and trust in his mercy, just as the hemorrhaging woman did. He will mend our broken hearts, ease searching hearts, and restore grieving hearts. My sons and I were wounded, even broken, but through mercy shown by others, and most importantly mercy shown to each other, we are binding up each other's wounds.

---

1. Reflect on your own experience with heartache. How did your body and emotions respond to that situation in your life? Did you receive mercy from anyone? How did your community respond to you?
2. Think of a time when a loved one experienced misery or misfortune. Were you able to empathize and extend help to alleviate

pain or provide comfort? Describe specific supportive ways to meet people in their pain.

3. Imagine you are the woman who hemorrhaged for twelve years. What about this interaction with Jesus would be the most impactful to you? Now, imagine you are one of the disciples or a member of the crowd or a high-ranking religious leader. What about this interaction would affect you most as a member of one of those groups?

Explore: Look up a local organization that aims to alleviate suffering in your community. Read a story from someone who has benefited from their acts of mercy. Donate to their work.

Chapter 16

Jesus Was Gentle

SUE M. DIAZ

> *Come to me, all you that are weary and are carrying heavy burdens, and I will give you rest. Take my yoke upon you, and learn from me, for I am gentle and humble in heart, and you will find rest for your souls. For my yoke is easy, and my burden is light.*
>
> —MATTHEW 11:28–30 (NRSVUE)

My mom's antique china cabinet brimmed with delicate treasures, memories, and mementos gathered across her lifetime. The figurines within the curved glass sides drew my daughter's attention more than any other object at Grandma's house, a menagerie of birdies and babies, bells and thimbles, and miniature teacups galore. When I was a child, these objects were untouchables. Decades later when my mom allowed my curious toddler to play with her precious porcelain, I fussed a bit. "Are you really going to let her play with your treasures?" With grandmotherly wisdom, she replied, "She will learn gentleness by enjoying the fragile things." This gentle teacher invited my daughter to find delight without fear.

In the quote from the book of Matthew at the beginning of this chapter, we read the words of another gentle teacher. Jesus invited his first-century audience to draw near without fear and learn from him how to find rest and security. His teaching credentials? Gentleness. In our day, we understand gentleness as something soft, nurturing, kind, and even grandmotherly—certainly not traits we seek when hiring a CEO, a team leader, or an athletic coach. Even saying the word *gentle* requires an exhale, a relaxing of the jaw. Jesus was gentle. But what did gentle mean in his day?

Developing the Meaning of Gentle

In ancient times, the word *gentle* conveyed a sense of setting aside one's entitled status and acting in an empathetic manner, perhaps even withholding harshness and offering grace instead. To be gentle meant to be unassuming. "A gentle answer turns away wrath," according to Proverbs 15:1. Gentleness in the first century meant laying down one's power in order to promote peace.

Unsurprisingly, gentleness is one of the fruits or virtues of the Holy Spirit, according to Paul in his letter to the Galatians (5:22–23). Gentleness, like the other virtues listed there, grows in us as evidence of the transforming power of Jesus. In a moment of anguish, Jesus wept over Jerusalem and longed to gather his people like a mother hen (Matthew 23:37). In Jesus's day, to be gentle meant to lay aside power and privilege, and to act with compassion as a parent toward a child.

Jesus Acts with Gentleness

In the gospel accounts, we witness this unassuming disposition of Jesus—his gentleness—in his actions and words. He showed compassion for the most vulnerable in his first-century society. He welcomed and played with children, spent time and conversed with women, consorted with so-called sinners, and touched the untouchable—the sick, the diseased, and the lepers. In a poignant scene in John 11, we learn that Jesus's friend Lazarus was sick and dying. By the time Jesus arrived, it was too late. His friend was gone, leaving behind his bereft sisters, Mary and Martha. In a tender moment, deeply moved by the pain and grief of his dear friends, gentle Jesus wept.

Jesus occasionally spoke of gentleness. In his famous Sermon on the Mount, Jesus described the unfathomably fabulous rewards for the most unlikely of people: the poor, the mournful, the persecuted, and even those who are gentle. According to this promise in Matthew 5:5, the gentle—the same Greek word Jesus uses to describe himself in Matthew 11:29—will inherit the earth! Here Jesus's words echo a beatitude from Psalm 37:11: "The meek shall inherit the land and delight themselves in abundant prosperity" (NRSVUE). No stranger to sorrow, Jesus also shared stories about lost coins, lost sheep, and a lost son. He understood loss, and his gentleness framed his compassionate response to those in grief. He grieved with the grieving, the essence of gentleness. In a most unassuming manner, Jesus entered into their sadness.

A gentle teacher, Jesus invited the weary and heavy laden to find rest by taking up his easy yoke. His instruction was clear: Come, take up my yoke, and learn from me (Matthew 11:28–30). The result of taking up this yoke was guaranteed rest for the soul. Gentle Jesus promised rest for anyone who followed him. In Jesus's day, a yoke was used to control working animals. Metaphorically, the yoke was also invoked to describe a teacher-student relationship. A person would figuratively yoke themselves to a particular rabbi for instruction. Eugene Peterson's paraphrase of this passage in *The Message* fleshes out what Jesus was offering here:

> Are you tired? Worn out? Burned out on religion? Come to me. Get away with me and you'll recover your life. I'll show you how to take a real rest. Walk with me and work with me—watch how I do it. Learn the unforced rhythms of grace. I won't lay anything heavy or ill-fitting on you. Keep company with me and you'll learn to live freely and lightly.

The gentle teacher's invitation to live freely without fear was very good news.

A Gentle Shepherd

In contrast to the "shame and blame" characteristically invoked by the social and religious culture of his day, Jesus was gentle, not judgmental. He had great compassion for the people who were "harassed and helpless, like sheep without a shepherd" (Matthew 9:36). He offered freedom to live in his pasture without electric fences. They could be free to learn his simple way of loving God and others. He would not coerce anyone into taking up his easy yoke. He never used shame to manipulate. He welcomed these "sheep" as they were—the hobbled, the lame, the blind, the infirm, the aged—tending to their brokenness and bondage, their conflicts and confusion. He loved them with gentleness, not judgment. He offered them security, not retaliation—rest for their souls.

Jesus never used shame to manipulate. He welcomed these "sheep" as they were.

Using this same beautiful metaphor, Jesus identified himself as the "Good Shepherd" in the gospel of John. Note the sacrificial aspect of gentleness in this passage: "I am the good shepherd. The good shepherd lays down his life for the sheep. . . . I know my own, and my own know me" (John 10:11, 14 NRSVUE). Jesus as the Good Shepherd has been a much-loved image throughout the millennia, featured in art, poetry, and music. For first-century audiences, the rest offered by the Good Shepherd Jesus was a theme well understood from the songs of King David. In Psalm 23 David, himself an experienced shepherd, writes from the perspective of a sheep. He recognizes the Lord as a gentle shepherd who offers his flock good grazing lands, still waters, peace even in the presence of danger, and the restoration of souls.

Gentleness, as modeled by shepherds, requires both grit and grace, strength and softness—all to secure the flock.

Jesus was a gentle shepherd, rabbi, and teacher. He didn't build fences to prevent his followers from leaving but gave them freedom. They were free to stay, rest, and delight in his protective, peaceful presence and under his light and easy yoke. Jesus was gentle with the vulnerable and outcast, and stern with his disciples when they tried to shoo them away. Gentle Jesus welcomed them. He welcomes us too.

Jesus is gentle now, just as he was then. His yoke is still easy; he still offers rest to those who feel outcast and weary of organized religion. He loves and accepts the vulnerable right where they are, just as they are. For some, it's a lifelong journey to navigate past shame. To those who choose to learn from him, he teaches the way of love—love for oneself and for one's neighbor. Jesus is still the Good Shepherd, whose "perfect love casts out fear" (1 John 4:18 NRSVUE). When I lived in fear of being punished by God, I was afraid to live fully and freely as myself, afraid to delight in anything. Fear and shame are miserable companions. Jesus still invites to a better journey: "Come to me. Get away with me and you'll recover your life" (Matthew 11:29 MSG).

In our most vulnerable space, in our deepest grief, in our utter failings, and in our weakest moments Jesus tenderly gathers the shattered and scattered pieces and reminds us that we belong to him. Even when we've broken the lovely things he's given for our enjoyment, he gives and forgives, again and again. My daughter learned gentleness from her gentle grandma; she had no fear of losing the love of the giver of good things. In much the same way, the ever-gentle Jesus invites us to draw near and freely delight in his company brimming over with gifts without fear or shame. When we are lost, afraid, or ashamed, he welcomes us without judgment, showering us with perfect love, the essence of gentleness.

---

1. How did you learn gentleness as a child? Is there a specific person who withheld harshness and offered you grace? Were you allowed to enjoy fragile things?
2. Have you "entered into" a friend's sadness? What is it like for you to grieve with the grieving?
3. Have you experienced weariness with organized religion? Does your faith community tire you out or teach you rhythms of rest? Are there aspects of church that feel "free" and "light"?

Explore: Make a list of things or activities that feel restorative to you. Reflect on how your body and emotions respond to these things and how they influence your spiritual health.

Chapter 17

Jesus Was Emotional

BECKY CASTLE MILLER

It is not possible to be spiritually mature while remaining emotionally immature.[1]

—Peter Scazzero

I grew up in Christian circles that viewed emotions as untrustworthy, so when I experienced an emotion, I either ignored it or tried to talk myself out of it. When I was sad about having to move again (and again and again) as a kid, I told myself that we were moving for my dad's ministry, so I was helping my family serve God by being happy about leaving my home and friends. I didn't allow myself to feel my sadness, or my homesickness, concerned that my uncomfortable emotions over doing God's will meant I was disobedient and unfaithful.

What about you? When you read the chapter title "Jesus Was Emotional," what was your initial reaction? Did you hear it as an insult to him, a denigration? Did you flinch and think, *But Jesus wasn't weak*?

Or, *Jesus wasn't driven by feelings.*

Or even, *Jesus wasn't sinful. How could he be emotional?*

What we think about Jesus's emotions, or lack of them, says a lot about how we view our own emotions. Maybe you value your emotions but aren't sure they're acceptable in Christian circles, so the news that Jesus was emotional sounds good to you, a relief.

But if you've been taught to distrust your emotions, you might distrust his, thus I thought that forcing myself into contented placidity and perfect acceptance was the best way to follow Jesus.

Then as a young adult, I actually read the Gospels, and I noticed that Jesus wasn't placid at all. Though some Christians today distrust emotions, the gospel writers present Jesus as an unequivocally emotional man. Stephen Voorwinde, in his book *Jesus's Emotions in the Gospels*, counts sixty of Jesus's emotional expressions.[2]

Gerald Hawthorne writes one of my favorite paragraphs about Jesus's human, emotional existence. He says the Gospels "stress the fact that Jesus was a human being . . . he was hungry, thirsty, and weary. They describe the full range of human emotions that Jesus felt—love, joy, grief, compassion, anger, gratitude, wonder . . . loneliness, perplexity, alarm, dismay, and despondency." Hawthorne records times that Jesus "expressed his feelings physically—he wept (John 11:35), he even wailed (Luke 19:41), he sighed (Mark 7:34), he groaned (8:12), he flashed angry glares at people (3:5), he spoke with annoyance in his voice (10:14) . . . broke out in a rage (John 11:33) . . . openly exulted (Luke 10:21), or cried aloud in utter desolation (Matthew 27:46)."[3]

If Jesus is emotional, that means I as his follower am free to be emotional too!

What Is Emotion?

Before we go on, let's establish some common understandings of terms. There are hundreds of definitions of "emotion," and a lot of things get attributed to emotion that aren't actually emotion at all.

Emotions are not animalistic impulses.

They are not weaknesses.

They are not the opposite of rational thought.

They are not physical urges.

Emotions are not sins.

Emotion is not the same thing as desire. Emotion is not even the same thing as feeling! Desire is to want something very much, and feeling is a physical sensation in our bodies. Emotion is neither of those things.

Here is the definition I am using for *emotion*: Emotions are the meaning our minds make out of our sensations and in our context. Emotions are the inspiration and fuel for our next actions.

When I was a kid listening to my parents tell us we were going to move again, I felt the prickle of tears in my nose, heaviness in my chest, and clenching in my stomach. In an instant, my mind related those sensations to other times I had felt similarly. My mind recalled the vocabulary I had been given through books and TV shows about characters moving or losing people and places they loved. All that put together constructed an instance of sadness. As a result of the emotion, my mind moved by body to take action toward my goals. I cried to release the tension and help my system rebalance. I committed to writing my friends regular letters to keep up the relationships. I looked for positives in the place we were moving to replace the sadness with anticipation.

Neuroscientist Lisa Feldman Barrett has developed this theory of constructed emotion. She speaks about humans "constructing" emotions rather than "experiencing" emotions.[4] Even though our minds construct an instance of an emotion in split seconds without conscious thought, we are actually constructing something, not just reacting out of nowhere due to inborn impulses. Our history and experiences, our language and vocabulary, and our caregivers and culture contribute to building our concept systems, including our emotion concepts. We can build, expand, and change our emotion concepts over time.

Jesus's Emotions

Jesus grew up with parents who spoke words to him and raised him in a culture, and this life experience built the emotion concepts he then used to construct emotions. The gospel writers recorded some of these emotional moments (and I'm sure there were plenty left unrecorded).

Jesus's incarnation means that he is fully human. As a human, he emoted like the rest of us. F. Scott Spencer writes, "Without full emotional capacity, Jesus can lay no claim to full participation in human experience. . . . The human capacity for emotion within Jesus is not cordoned off in some separate compartment from his divine character. . . . Whatever he feels in the Gospels, he feels as the unitary God-and-Man."[5]

As a human, Jesus emoted like the rest of us.

As we study these accounts of his life, his emotions can serve as models for us, influencing the emotion concept system our own minds are constantly building. As we observe Jesus's emotions, our own emotions are being shaped, preparing us to respond more like Jesus in our own circumstances and experiences. This passing on of emotion concepts is a microcosm of the discipleship process, so I call this "discipling our emotions."

Let's look at two of Jesus's emotions and then consider what this can teach us as his disciples.

Joy

> "The seventy-two returned with joy . . . At that time Jesus, full of joy through the Holy Spirit . . ." (Luke 10:17, 21)

Jesus sent seventy-two disciples out in pairs to practice the ministry he gave them. They returned with positive reports, the dialogue and descriptions infused with lighthearted emotions. Jesus talks about triumph over the enemy and tells the disciples to rejoice that their names are written in heaven. He is talking about being glad or joyful and telling them what the object of their emotion should be. He thanks the Father and celebrates his relationship with the Father, which shows gratitude. He tells them their eyes are blessed (or happy) to be witnessing these events. Jesus appears to be constructing instances of happiness or joy along with success and gratefulness. He wanted his disciples to be successful in the mission he gave them, and they were. There is a place for joy in kingdom work, both his joy and ours. It's a good thing to enjoy the work of ministry.

Zeal

> So he made a whip out of cords, and drove all from the temple courts, both sheep and cattle; he scattered the coins of the money changers and overturned their tables. . . . His disciples remembered that it is written: "Zeal for your house will consume me." (John 2:15, 17)

When Jesus sees people turning the temple into a market, he makes (not borrows or buys, *makes!*) a whip, throws around their coins, and knocks over their tables. He screams at them to get out. Voorwinde calls him "livid" and writes, "It is often said that Jesus was angry when he cleared the temple. But anger is too tame a word."[6]

It's Jesus's disciples who name his emotion. In Barrett's language, they are *perceiving* the emotion he is *constructing*. Their own emotion concepts are giving them names for what they are seeing in Jesus, and their best guess for what he is emoting is "zeal." The Old Testament reference to zeal here (quoted by John from Psalm 69:9) is a good example of how our emotion concepts are formed. When our culture or religion gives us words and ideas around emotion, we can then construct those emotions in ourselves later. This fervor for the protection and holiness of God's dwelling place is an emotion we can learn from Jesus.

What Does This Mean for Us as Disciples?

We can look at Jesus, our King and friend, through the lens of his emotions to come to a new appreciation for what he did for us. Voorwinde reminds us that "Jesus went through deep emotional pain and spiritual trauma for the redemption of his people."[7]

We can find comfort and solidarity in Jesus's emotions. Counselor K. J. Ramsey writes, "If you are feeling crushed by pain or fear, go to the Garden. Bear witness to Jesus's tears. Notice how his fear spilled from his body as blood . . . The God of the Garden, cross, and grave is the God who knows your name and is with you in your pain."[8] We can look at Jesus's emotions as an example to follow. Instead of suppressing our emotions, ignoring them, disliking them, or judging them, what if we embraced them? What if we realized we could change them, gradually over time, to become more and more Christlike, just like every other area of our lives as disciples? The more we learn emotion concepts from Jesus, the more likely we will be to construct Christlike emotions in our best and worst moments.

As I have learned to disciple my emotions, I am growing to realize they are not a detriment to my spiritual life. They are a beautiful part of the vibrant life of emotional and spiritual maturity I'm growing into as a follower of our emotional Jesus.

---

1. How did you see emotions expressed when you were young?
2. Do the definitions of *joy* and *zeal* from this essay make sense to you? When have you experienced these emotions? Have you seen a range of emotions expressed in your faith community?
3. Is there someone in your life who is good at expressing their emotions? How did they learn to embrace their emotions in Christlike ways?

Explore: Watch a favorite movie or particular scene from a movie. Write out why you like this movie and what emotions you experience through it.

Chapter 18

Jesus Was Subversive

SARAH BUCY KLINGLER

My kingdom is not of this world.
—JOHN 18:36

Like many people my age who grew up in white evangelical spaces in the 1980s and '90s, my understanding of Revelation was shaped by the *Left Behind* book series. So when I took a class on Revelation at Northern Seminary, I faced a book of the Bible I had previously avoided at all costs. I had heard all about the rapture, the Antichrist, and the mark of the beast, and although I had trusted Christ as my Savior at a young age, I was still extremely fearful of being "left behind." Imagine my shock to learn that Revelation is not mainly about predicting the future and understanding specific details of the end times but rather is a letter to seven churches in Asia Minor calling them to worship Jesus alone, the conquering Lamb of God.

These churches were caught up in the Roman Empire—its love of status, wealth, and military might, and its unquestioning cultic worship of the emperor as lord. The author of Revelation, John of Patmos, "summons readers to life-encompassing worship that is an alternative to worship of emperor and empire. A litany early in John's vision says followers of the Lamb are a kingdom and priests serving our God. That is political language, calling followers of Jesus Christ to alternative allegiance and alternative identity."[1] John didn't invent this alternative allegiance and identity. Rather, it was a direct reflection of Jesus of Nazareth, who didn't come through the normal channels of power, as would be expected of the Messiah, the Son of God. Instead, he subverted the power structures of his day and showed his followers a different way.

A Subversive Birth

The events surrounding the birth of Christ set the stage for this revolutionary new type of kingdom reign and rule, which looked nothing like what the world expected. Jesus was born to Mary, an ordinary young teenager, likely in a simple family home in Bethlehem. His bed? Not an ornate cradle handcrafted from the finest materials but a feeding trough filled with hay. His clothes? Not a silk, hand-spun nightgown but strips of "swaddling clothes" (Luke 2:7 KJV). His attendants? Not servants and soldiers but farm animals. Nothing about this screamed power, authority, or might because God's power, authority, and might don't resemble those of any empire. It was an epic reversal in which God humbled himself to become one of us to show us the way to truly live as humans, not through power over others but through servanthood.

There were clues right from the start of his earthly life that Jesus was no simple, ordinary baby. First, there was the angel who appeared to the shepherds, heralding good news of the birth of the Messiah, the Lord, which would bring joy to all people. This angel was joined by a company of angels, a heavenly host who worshipped and praised God for this newborn king (Luke 2:8–14). We might not recognize it in our cultural context, but in ancient Rome words like *good news* and *lord* were often associated with the emperor and used in imperial proclamations to recognize his power.[2] These terms were purposefully co-opted by the New Testament authors to describe the King of Kings, who alone is worthy of our worship and allegiance. The borrowing of the language of empire was subversive, and it would ultimately be seen by that empire as the first in a long line of treasonous acts by the followers of Jesus.

Further acknowledgment of the good news of Jesus's lordship came from the Magi from the East, who had witnessed a star that they believed to be a sign indicating a royal birth. They traveled a long distance, bearing lavish gifts to pay homage to this new king, and ended up subverting a possible assassination attempt by disregarding King Herod's request for them to let him know the exact location of the baby Jesus. Herod was so threatened by this potential rival to his throne that he ordered the barbaric slaughter of all baby boys two years old and younger in the region. Having been warned in a dream of Herod's plan, Mary and Joseph fled with Jesus as refugees to Egypt, where they remained until the death of King Herod (Matthew 2:1–18). This was just the start of Jesus's subversive life.

A Subversive Ministry

Through the Gospel authors' description of his ministry years, we see Jesus spent very little time rubbing shoulders with those in positions of authority. He did not frequent halls of power or surround himself with wealthy, upper-class, well-positioned people. Instead, Jesus spent his time out on the hillsides, on the highways and byways, in the homes of sinners, and in spaces where no respectable person at that time would have entered. He surrounded himself with those who would have been considered the ordinary and even the marginalized. This was not popular in a world concerned with attaining honor, status, and power. Even Jesus's disciples, those who knew him intimately and learned from his example, yearned for a taste of worldly authority. One day, some of them began arguing about who was the greatest in the group and who deserved to sit in the places of honor beside Jesus, in what they assumed would be his earthly kingdom in Jerusalem. Instead, Jesus reminded them of the upside-down way of living in God's kingdom.

> You know that among the gentiles those whom they recognize as their rulers lord it over them, and their great ones are tyrants over them. But it is not so among you; instead, whoever wishes to become great among you must be your servant, and whoever wishes to be first among you must be slave of all. For the Son of Man came not to be served but to serve and to give his life a ransom for many. (Mark 10:42–45 NRSVue)

At times Jesus refused to play along with the religious rulers, many of whom he criticized for being so consumed with judging others, adding layer upon layer to God's law that they grew too busy to love and care about people. They were threatened by Jesus, who spoke with authority, cast out demons, healed the sick, and drew crowds around him wherever he went. He wasn't afraid to heal on the Sabbath or to touch those considered "unclean." He hadn't come to abolish the law but to fulfill it (Matthew 5:17), and he summed up the entire law with these two commands: love God and love your neighbor as yourself (Mark 12:30–31). Add to this the fact that he refused to worship at the feet of the empire, condemned riches, and claimed to be the Messiah (Matthew 19:24; Luke 4:16–22; John 4:25–26; 18:36), and it is no wonder he became enemy number one of the ruling powers in Jewish society. We see all throughout the gospels the lengths that the Jewish leaders went to in order to trap and trick Jesus. Suffice it to say, he was always at odds with those wielding earthly power (as first demonstrated in his response to Satan tempting him in the wilderness), and his life was often in danger (Matthew 26:1–5; John 11:45–57).

Jesus reminded them of the upside-down way of living in God's kingdom.

In Luke's gospel we see the long journey (beginning in 9:51 and culminating in 19:46) Jesus took getting to Jerusalem, the seat of power for the political and religious leaders of Judea. He did not ride in on a war horse surrounded by men with weapons ready to go to battle for him. Instead, he rode in on a lowly donkey's colt, representing peace and a different kind of kingdom. It wasn't governors, kings, or priests who greeted him with shouts of "Hosanna!," "Blessed is he who comes in the name of the Lord!," and "Blessed is the king of Israel!" (John 12:13). No, it was the ordinary people who also expected him to initiate a certain type of kingdom, one that would overthrow the Romans once and for all. What they instead found was a King who refused to give in to the lust for earthly power—which oppresses, abuses, and kills—and gave himself over to those earthly powers to be interrogated, beaten, and crucified as a subversive criminal. The religious leaders handed him over, and the empire hung him on a cross as the King of the Jews. Yet we know this wasn't the end. Earthly power is no match for heavenly power, and Christ was raised and reigns victorious to this day.

Following in Jesus's Subversion

As I think about how Jesus subverted the power structures during his time on earth, I wonder whether Christians today in the West truly understand how radical this calling is that has been placed on those of us who claim him as Lord. We, too, must stand against the power structures of our day—whether political, military, economic, or religious—and choose instead to lay down our power, to serve others, and to live lives of radical love for our neighbor. Sadly, what we see far too often is that "much of Christendom today seems less interested in seeing as Jesus saw, less inclined to enter in, and far more interested in gaining power. We have acquired fame, money, status, reputation, and our own little kingdoms."[3] Are we swayed by the little kingdoms of our time, such as patriarchy, nationalism, denominationalism, or even by the temptation to make our own church the center of the universe? Or are we Christ-centered—Christocentric—in our life and ministry? Just like the churches in Revelation, we, too, must be reminded that our full allegiance lies with the true King, who gave his life so that oppression, injustice, and all the evil tied to worldly power would be defeated.

At the beginning of this chapter, I shared a bit about my experience with Revelation and how I've come to see it differently—namely, through the lens of worship and allegiance to the Lamb. This worship and allegiance subvert all the ways the world and its powers try to vie for those very same things. The question becomes, How do we live this out practically?

For me, one way I've tried to lean into Jesus's model of the upside-down kingdom is in the type of church I've chosen to attend. By worldly standards, and even by the standards of some American Christians, my church wouldn't be considered significant or effective. We don't have many people attending on Sunday. We don't have much money. We don't have a pastor with a huge platform. We don't offer tons of programs. And we don't have a fancy building with a café. But what we do have is a diverse community of Jesus seekers who partner with local organizations and ministries doing incredible work in our urban community to minister to people who are often forgotten and overlooked, everything from addiction recovery programs to youth centers to gospel hip-hop concerts and so much more. During the warmer months we have church in a small local park on a main thoroughfare. People come in off the street for a coffee and a doughnut and worship with us briefly or stay and become part of our community. Some have even gotten baptized in a stainless-steel tub right there on the boulevard. Sometimes being faithful followers of a subversive Jesus simply means reexamining the priorities of our church to see whether they align with the priorities of our King.

---

1. Does your faith community highlight Jesus's birth as a subversive moment? If someone curious about Christianity asked you about Jesus's birth, how would you describe it?

2. When have you encountered authorities or power structures that do not serve others sacrificially and instead are self-serving? Have you ever seen someone model power by giving it away in radical ways?
3. Are you gifted or skilled in a particular type of service for others? Does your service subvert typical power structures in your local community? How can we encourage serving others?

Explore: Read or listen to a biography of a Christian who subverted the authorities or power structures that surrounded them in order to serve others as Jesus did. A great place to start would be to pick up *Strange Glory: A Life of Dietrich Bonhoeffer* by Charles Marsh or *The Spirit of Justice: True Stories of Faith, Race, and Resistance* by Jemar Tisby. Reflect on how your body and emotions respond to their stories.

Chapter 19

Jesus Was Compassionate

CODY MATCHETT

> *The emotion which we should naturally expect to find most frequently attributed to that Jesus whose whole life was a mission of mercy, and whose ministry was so marked by deeds of beneficence that it was summed up in the memory of his followers as a going through the land "doing good" (Acts 11.38), is no doubt "compassion." In point of fact, this is the emotion which is most frequently attributed to him.*[1]
>
> —B. B. WARFIELD

What motivates or moves you?

The answer to this question may not be as clear as you might think. Motives are messy. Sometimes our motives are pure, noble, and clear. At other times they are selfish, tainted, and convoluted. Worse still, at any given moment we are crushed by the conflicting nature of our motives.

Jesus Was Moved by What He Saw

What about Jesus? What motivated him? In Matthew 9 we are offered a window into the ministry of Jesus as he teaches in the synagogues, proclaims the gospel of the kingdom, and cures every disease and sickness (verse 35). Matthew's summary of Jesus's ministry serves as a key transition point in the narrative, which is followed by a statement regarding Jesus's motivation: *compassion*.[2] When Jesus "saw the crowds, he had *compassion* on them, because they were harassed and helpless, like sheep without a shepherd" (verse 36). Jesus's response is described by the emotional Greek verb *splanchnizomai*, which refers to an affectionate and warm response to those in need.[3] The term is challenging to translate into English: "compassion, pity, sympathy, and fellow feeling all convey part of it, but 'his heart went out' perhaps represents more fully the emotional force of the underlying metaphor of a 'gut response.'"[4]

In other words, Jesus's heart *went out* to them. He was moved by emotional concern because of their state of profound distress.[5] The multitudes were like sheep without a shepherd, lacking guidance, leadership, or care. The language conjures images of helpless sheep distressed on account of being left at the whim of weather conditions, lack of provision, and predators. The imagery also recalls a myriad of similar passages in the Hebrew Bible that reference Israel as God's flock and Israel's leaders as shepherds (e.g., Numbers 27:17; Ezekiel 34:5).[6] Jesus was compassionate toward the people because they were abandoned, left without provision, food, and care. According to one expert on the book of Matthew, compassion is *the* word that describes the "Jesus of the gospel stories in a nutshell."[7] In the end, compassion seems to be an emotional reaction, eliciting heart-stirring care that culminates in effective action.

Jesus's heart *went out* to them.

Moreover, as alluded to above, compassion is first and foremost an *emotional reaction*, a gut response that emerges from deep within.[8] Compassion is a disruptive, heart-wrenching experience that moves us deeply on account of the circumstances of others. In Matthew 14 we read again that when Jesus saw the great crowds that followed him on foot from the towns, he "had *compassion* on them and healed their sick" (verse 14). Jesus *saw* the crowds, his eyes open to the brokenness and heartbreak experienced by other human beings. Jesus *saw* those who had *not* been clothed, strengthened, healed, bound up, or brought back. Simply seeing those enduring suffering elicited a deep visceral response in Jesus. Walter Rauschenbusch in his book *Christianity and the Social Crisis*, commenting on the perception and vision of the prophets, puts it this way, "They looked open-eyed at the events about them and then turned to the inner voice of God to interpret what they saw."[9]

Jesus Was Moved to Respond

Compassion, however, does not remain as an emotional reaction we feel inside ourselves but moves to *heart-stirring care* through our response. Seeing the dire condition of the people around him moved Jesus into action. After Jesus saw the crowds and felt for the people, he wanted to care for them. In Matthew 15 he called his disciples and said to them, "I have *compassion* for these people; they have already been with me three days and have nothing to eat. I do not want to send them away hungry, or they may collapse on the way" (verse 32). Jesus does not dismiss the gut reaction or blame the people for their lack of responsibility and foresight, but instead he allows the feelings to move from his gut to his heart. Jesus does not despise but instead accepts. He does not blame but instead provides. He does not dismiss but instead feels. Jesus does not view the people in light of what they have done or failed to do, but he views them in light of their suffering and need. As noted by Dietrich Bonhoeffer in his *Letters and Papers from Prison*:

> We must learn to regard human beings less in terms of what they do and neglect to do and more in terms of what they suffer. The only fruitful relation to human beings—particularly to the weak among them—is love, that is, the will to enter into

> and to keep community with them. God did not hold human beings in contempt but became human for their sake.[10]

After moving from emotional reaction to heart-stirring care, compassion must culminate in *effective action*. In Matthew 20 as Jesus was leaving Jericho followed by a massive crowd, two blind men were shouting: "Lord, Son of David, have mercy on us!" (verse 30). The crowd wanted the men to shut up, but they got louder, shouting again, "Lord, Son of David, have mercy on us!" (verse 31). Matthew writes that Jesus stood still, summoned them to come forward, and asked, "What do you want me to do for you?" (verse 32). Jesus not only stopped, heard, saw, felt, and was pierced to his heart, but he was moved to action. The question Jesus asked the men assumes not only an emotional gut reaction to the men and heart-stirring care but also the intention to move toward effective action. Jesus enters into their situation, pain, and need in order to remedy and rectify their circumstances. Henri Nouwen, Donald McNeill, and Douglas Morrison put it this way:

> Compassion asks us to go where it hurts, to enter into places of pain, to share in brokenness, fear, confusion, and anguish. Compassion challenges us to cry out with those in misery, to mourn with those who are lonely, to weep with those in tears. Compassion requires us to be weak with the weak, vulnerable with the vulnerable, and powerless with the powerless. Compassion means full immersion in the condition of being human.[11]

Jesus was willing to immerse himself completely within the human condition and to enter into the plight of humanity because he was moved by deep emotional concern. As Jesus took on human nature, he became the very embodiment of compassion that led him to heal, redeem, and restore.

Compassion Moves Us

To follow in the footsteps of the compassionate one, we must *first* slow down and open our eyes and ears to the world around us: "Blessed are your eyes because they see, and your ears because they hear" (Matthew 13:16). *Second*, we must allow ourselves to experience fully the visceral emotions that emerge from slowing down, seeing, and hearing. *Third*, we must not repress or dismiss these emotions but instead allow them to plant seeds deep within our hearts. *Finally*, we must allow the seeds of care to germinate and grow, until they bloom into effective action.

What moves you? Jesus was moved by compassion.

Jesus experienced emotional reactions, which elicited heart-stirring care that culminated in effective action. Jesus entered in and experienced the misery of the other and was compelled to bring healing to every nation, tribe, people, and tongue by every means within his power.[12] As noted by Nouwen, McNeil, and Morrison, "When Jesus was moved to compassion, the source of all life trembled, the ground of all life burst open, and the abyss of God's immense, inexhaustible, and unfathomable tenderness revealed itself."[13]

May our compassion cause life to burst open, and may the immense, inexhaustible, and unfathomable tenderness of God be revealed through us by the power of Holy Spirit.

---

1. How do your body and emotions respond to Matthew 9:36 when Jesus "saw the crowds, he had compassion for them, because they were harassed and helpless, like sheep without a shepherd"? Have you felt harassed and helpless? Do you sense Jesus's deep compassion for you?
2. Does your faith community express compassion for others through "heart-stirring care"? What does that care look like? Are there particular ways your church is uniquely suited to provide a specific type of effective care that is needed in your community?

3. How does your daily schedule affect your perception of those around you who experience heartaches? Do you have time to see the difficulties other people experience? Does your faith community promote slowness in this way?

Explore: Spend time milling around in a place with people from your community (a mall, a parade, a festival, a coffee shop, etc.). Give yourself time to people watch and pray for individuals as they cross your path. If the Holy Spirit prompts you, strike up a conversation and ask someone about their life.

Chapter 20

Jesus Was a Friend to Sinners and Outcasts

PETER GREEN

Mercy triumphs over judgment.
—JAMES 2:13

I was raised in a fundamentalist church and learned early on that holiness was defined by the list of things you didn't do, such as drinking alcohol, smoking, gambling, listening to rock music, and dancing. At one point, our church took over a smaller church whose pastor had died, and most of us were shocked to find out that in that church, square dances were considered okay for young Christians. I realized then that each church has its own list of "sins," its own boundary lines that help us avoid getting anywhere near the *real* ones. I learned that sins and sinners should be kept at a distance for fear our holiness would be ruined.

"Love the sinner but hate the sin." Like me, you may have heard this overused Christian cliché many times. In recent years it has been used frequently in the debate over homosexuality, but in addition to not being in the Bible, the phrase has been shown to lead more to hate than to love.[1] Those on the receiving end of this phrase generally do not feel the love, as the hatred of sin tends to overshadow any professed love of the sinner. For example, in my own church I have witnessed too many young people who are gay feel rejected by God because they have been rejected by fellow Christians. Does a desire to be holy have to result in an overt hatred of certain sins? Is that what holiness is? Shunning or shaming sinners in case we are contaminated or led astray by their sin? The answer lies in the example of Jesus, who, according to the author of Hebrews, is the "exact representation" of God (1:3). In other words, if you want to know what God is like, look at Jesus. We often skip past how Jesus treated sinners so we can focus on how sinners responded to Jesus. Maybe we should slow down and give Jesus's actions more consideration. How did Jesus treat sinners when he was on earth?

Holiness, Grace, and Tax Collectors

In the time of Jesus, the Jewish religious leaders promoted a system of ritual practices and rules meant to protect worshippers of God from anything that might defile them and prevent them from living a holy life. At the top of the list was eating with sinners. In the ancient Mediterranean world, eating together was a social event that symbolized acceptance of those with whom you were eating. A good Pharisee would not be caught dead dining with a sinner, especially the worst of sinners—tax collectors and prostitutes.

How did Jesus treat sinners when he was on earth?

Tax collectors were among the most despised and hated people in Judea. Governed by the orders of local magistrates working under the thumb of the Roman Empire, tax collectors were public contractors who often received a bad reputation due to their association with their oppressive bosses, not to mention the fact that their income derived directly from the taxes they collected. Prostitutes were also at the bottom of the social hierarchy, as Judaism had a strict code of sexual ethics. Into this world came Jesus, and instead of shunning the tax collectors and prostitutes, he seemed drawn to them and, horror of horrors, frequently shared meals with them. Not only that, he actually called a tax collector, Levi (Matthew), to be one of his twelve disciples. All three of the Synoptic Gospels record the calling of Levi and emphasize the scandal it caused among the Pharisees and religious leaders. Mark recorded the story like this:

> While Jesus was having dinner at Levi's house, many tax collectors and sinners were eating with him and his disciples, for there were many who followed him. When the teachers of the law who were Pharisees saw him eating with the sinners and tax collectors, they asked his disciples: "Why does he eat with tax collectors and sinners?" (Mark 2:15–16)

The phrase "there were many who followed him" is interesting, as it suggests that tax collectors were particularly attracted to Jesus. Why might that have been? We know that Jesus preached a message of repentance. The first words Jesus preached in Matthew's gospel were: "Repent, for the kingdom of heaven has come near" (Matthew 4:17). Jesus had even higher moral standards than the Pharisees. He says in the Sermon on the Mount that "unless your righteousness surpasses that of the Pharisees and the teachers of the law, you will certainly not enter the kingdom of heaven" (Matthew 5:20). It is hard to believe that tax collectors and prostitutes would be inviting Jesus to their homes for dinner if that were his only message.

Since tax collectors were already despised by most people, why would they want someone else telling them how evil they were? Most of them were very aware of their less than glowing social reputations. In Jesus's parable of the Pharisee and the tax collector praying in the temple (18:9–14), the tax collector was acutely aware of his sinfulness. He didn't need anyone reminding him of it. What he needed was mercy and forgiveness.

So why did tax collectors and prostitutes want to hang out with Jesus? According to Luke, Jesus claimed in his first sermon that he was fulfilling the prophecy in Isaiah by coming to preach "good news to the poor" and "proclaim the year of the Lord's favor" (Luke 4:18–19). This good news began with a change of heart (repentance) but was also a message of grace, which made it attractive to those who were regarded as outcasts in society. Jesus demonstrated what Craig Blomberg calls "contagious holiness."[2] Rather than fearing pollution from sinners, Jesus went into dark places as the "light of the world" (John 8:12), and the darkness did not overcome the light (1:5). Instead, his holiness rubbed off onto others and often brought transformation. As Blomberg puts it: "He does not assume that he will be defiled by associating with corrupt people. Rather, his purity can rub off on them and change them for the better. Cleanliness, he believes, is even more 'catching' than uncleanness; morality more influential than immorality."[3] For those who see holiness as separating themselves from the world and avoiding dens of iniquity in order to keep themselves "from being polluted by the world" (James 1:27), the thought of Jesus voluntarily dining with unrepentant sinners from the bottom of society can be challenging. But it seems Jesus did just that.

Mercy and Friendship

The Gospels do not say that Jesus's outcast dinner companions were *former* tax collectors or *ex*-sinners. Nor do they say whether these figures ever stopped doing what they were doing. The only two tax collectors who change their ways in the New Testament are Matthew, who abandoned his profession to follow Jesus, and Zacchaeus, the chief tax collector who responded to Jesus inviting himself over by saying he would give away half his possessions to the poor and pay back four times the amount he had overcharged anyone (which presumably made a large dent in his income).

But if the other tax collectors and prostitutes Jesus was eating with had already left their stigmatized professions, then surely there would not have been a scandal over Jesus eating with them. In fact, if they had changed their ways, Jesus would have likely been viewed as a sort of hero in reforming so many wicked people, at least in the eyes of the common people. But he wasn't. Jesus himself alluded to the fact that his friendship with sinners caused widespread offense when he said: "For John came neither eating or drinking, and they say, 'He has a demon.' The Son of Man came eating and drinking, and they say, 'Here is a glutton and a drunkard, a friend of tax collectors and sinners'" (Matthew 11:18–19). The phrase "a glutton and drunkard" is a reference to Deuteronomy 21:20, which is about rebellious sons deserving death, so obviously Jesus's critics took great offense at his actions.

Jesus owned the "friend of sinners" tag. He did not just tolerate these sinners or see them simply as souls to be saved. It is likely that Jesus saw his dining with the tax collectors and sinners as a prophetic action in line with the tradition of Hebrew prophets before him, who did all kinds of strange things to make a point. But Jesus actually seemed to enjoy their company, and they certainly enjoyed his, as they kept inviting him back.

Why was that? We will never know for sure, but it seems that Jesus saw them for who they were and valued them as human beings made in the image of God. John highlighted this characteristic of Jesus when he said, "The law was given through Moses; grace and truth came through Jesus Christ" (John 1:17). Jesus saw past people's social statuses and demonstrated grace and mercy like no one else.

Victims of Injustice

One important factor of the time was that quite a few of the lower-level tax collectors and prostitutes were slaves with no control over their situations, entangled within broader structures of injustice and sin.[4]

Jesus told the woman caught in adultery to "go and sin no more"

(John 8:11 NLT) because she had the freedom to make a moral choice, and this is typical of Jesus's call to righteous living (Matthew 5:20). We have no record, however, of Jesus saying the same thing to a prostitute. The story of the sinful woman who anointed Jesus at the house of Simon the Pharisee (Luke 7:36–50) comes straight after Jesus agrees that he is a friend of tax collectors and "sinners." What is interesting is that at the end of the encounter, Jesus told the woman, "Your sins are forgiven . . . go in peace."

Jesus saw past people's social statuses and demonstrated grace and mercy like no one else.

Slavery was common in the first century, with around 250,000 humans being sold as slaves in the Roman Forum every year.[5] Slaves were at the bottom of society and had few rights. They were forced into sex acts with their masters and often with his friends or customers. Those slaves who responded to the message of Jesus were usually not free to change their lifestyle and most likely were forced to continue to perform these sexual acts. Likewise, tax collection was not a profession that anyone wanted to do, and so chief tax collectors (like Zacchaeus) would often utilize slaves to do the actual collecting of the tax. Despite being despised for doing so, these slaves were not in a position to walk away from their profession.

Biblical scholar Mark Powell suggests Jesus saw the dilemma these unfortunate people were caught in and, in true Jesus style, had mercy triumph over judgment (James 2:13).[6] In situations where people could not extract themselves from lives of sin and suffered constant shame, Jesus extended grace. That does not mean he compromised his own moral standards, but he accommodated the fact that we live in a broken world, just as God himself accommodated humans in the Torah by allowing divorce, polygamy, slavery, and various other immoral or less than ideal practices.

Missionaries today face this situation in cultures that have practices that are deeply problematic for Christians, such as polygamy and the oppression of women, but most missionaries have learned to let the indigenous Christians work out how to deal with these issues and to trust the Spirit to guide them. Pete Greig gives a modern example of this in his book *Dirty Glory*, where he relates the story of a West African girl living on the Spanish island of Ibiza who was saved and became a worship leader yet remained trapped in prostitution.[7] She was an undocumented immigrant who owed large amounts of money to her madam, and she was supporting her family back in Africa with her earnings. Considering the ways Jesus responded to those who were seen as sinners presents us with a new perspective. Who are we to judge those whom Christ has saved who find themselves victims of unjust systems that they are unable to escape from?

Offering Friendship

Jesus's friendship with sinners may be just as shocking to us as it was to his contemporaries. It challenges those of us who would be quick to judge others without knowing the circumstances of the person we are judging. Receiving the friendship of Jesus is also a surprising message of grace to those of us who live in shame and feel we are unworthy of love: Jesus has a special place in his heart for those of us whom the world has written off.

We must ask ourselves, Will people know such love by the way we live our lives? Do we avoid those who participate in our list of sins, or do we imitate Jesus and go out of our way to be friends with sinners and outcasts?

I believe the phrase "love the sinner but hate the sin" should be retired from use, or at least modified to "love the sinner and hate the sin in your own life." Jesus taught his disciples not to judge others (Matthew 7:1), and Paul warned against judging fellow believers, as they are God's servants and "their own master will judge whether they stand or fall. And with the Lord's help, they will stand and receive his approval" (Romans 14:4 NLT).

What would happen if instead of focusing on other people's sins, we loved God with all our heart, soul, mind, and strength (Mark 12:30) and were so full of the Holy Spirit that we practiced "contagious holiness" when we went about loving our neighbor? What if we followed the example of Christ and went out of our way to have a meal with sinners and outcasts with a view to showing God's love to them? Would the marginalized and outcasts, rather than feeling condemned, be attracted to a better way of life and want to follow Jesus?

As Craig Blomberg concludes in his study of table fellowship with sinners, "Our desperately lost and hurting world demands no less!"[8] I want my love for God to be contagious to saints *and* sinners, and that means spending time together.

---

1. How do you feel when you read "Those on the receiving end of this phrase ["love the sinner but hate the sin"] generally do not feel the love, as the hatred of sin tends to overshadow any professed love of the sinner"? Have you ever been put in the role of "sinner"?
2. Who in your local community has little power to change their situation? How can your local community support changes in power dynamics?
3. How do you define *friendship*? What is necessary to form a friendship? Do you have significant friendships with people who live and believe differently than you do?

Explore: Invite some friends over and have a good time. Don't make anyone a "project"; just appreciate each other's company and care for your friends as people you enjoy being around. Reflect on what it's like to follow Jesus in this way.

Chapter 21

Jesus Was for Women

SUSY FLORY

My whole life is leaning toward him, questing for him,
striving to break down the walls inside that shelter
me from his gaze.[1]

—Frederica Mathewes-Green

I grew up a church girl in the San Francisco Bay Area. While the surrounding cities were bastions of peace, free love, and lots of tie-dye, our church was very conservative in both theology and behavioral rules. No alcohol, smoking, rock music, short shorts, or any other controversial behavior or habits allowed. Questions were generally discouraged.

I loved learning and was always the first to raise my hand and answer my Sunday school teacher's questions or study the names of the books of the Bible diligently so I could win at Bible competitions such as "sword drills." But as I approached my teen years, the thrill of being the smartest and the best began to wear off as my teachers and other leaders grew tired of my enthusiasm and my knack for remembering stories and facts, and I think I became more of an annoyance than anything else.

I'll never forget one Sunday evening when I arrived at church with my dad. I was about fourteen years old and dressed in a brand-new outfit that I loved: brown corduroy pants, vest, and a long-sleeve shirt underneath. My hair was carefully blow-dried—which, in the days before hair gel and mousse, only made it curlier—so I looked like I had a brown labradoodle puppy on my head. I was still getting used to my new five-foot-ten tall body, so I walked and moved with an awkward gait and most of the time felt very self-conscious. But on this night everything coordinated and, for once, I felt like I was in style.

My dad pushed open the heavy front door of the church, and we walked through into warmth and light. We stood for a minute, side by side, as a gray-haired man I didn't recognize approached. I found out later he worked for the denomination and came by our church periodically to see how things were going.

"Frank, how are you doing?" he boomed, hand extended. They talked for a minute as I hung back, feeling uncomfortable. Then my dad moved to the side as the man stepped toward me and practically shouted, "Who is this fine young man? Introduce me to your son!"

If ever I wished I could rewind and delete a piece of real life, that was the time. I didn't know what to say. Neither did my dad.

Oh, that I would've had the guts to say, brightly and just as loud, "Hello. I'm a girl, and my name is Susy." But I was busy shrinking back and dying of shame while my dad explained I was his daughter, not his son.

However, it was what happened next that killed me—one of those small moments that seems insignificant and harmless but grows in power over time. I can still see it, hear it, and feel it. Because as soon as the man realized I was a young woman, his face went flat. All interest gone.

He was not embarrassed at his gaffe. Instead, he seemed . . . disappointed. He had walked up to my dad, seeing a clean-cut, handsome, and strong young man, and he'd been excited. Maybe because he'd identified a future leader of the church? I don't know. It still haunts me.

I loved Jesus with all my heart and wanted to learn everything I could about him. I still do. But I began to ask myself, *Was Jesus for women too?* The easy answer is, yes! For starters, he had a beloved mother, Mary, who stayed to the end and beyond. The Gospels and

Acts tell us of the many other women in his life who were relatives, friends, supporters, followers, students, and disciples.

But one stands out to me—Mary Magdalene.

A Female Disciple

We don't know many facts about her life, although there's been much speculation over the last two thousand years. Her actions are recorded on only two occasions in the New Testament. The first introduction to Mary Magdalene is in the gospel of Luke. Jesus and a group of followers are traveling the countryside and "proclaiming the good news of the kingdom of God." Here's a description of Jesus's followers:

> The Twelve were with him, and also some women who had been cured of evil spirits and diseases: Mary (called Magdalene) from whom seven demons had come out; Joanna the wife of Chuza, the manager of Herod's household; Susanna; and many others. These women were helping to support them out of their own means. (Luke 8:1–3)

What stands out most to me in this brief passage is that Mary Magdalene had been demon possessed. Some modern commentators explain away the Bible's mentions of demonic possession as simply mental illness, but demons or evil spirits are mentioned sixty-three times in the Gospels alone and were understood as beings or forces that clearly intended to bring serious harm to the people they were plaguing. Later in the same chapter, a demon-possessed man who lived across the lake from Galilee was likewise delivered by Jesus. If Mary Magdalene's condition had been in any way similar, her experience must have been horrific, and she had likely been an outcast. But her life, which must have been in shambles, was restored. She responded with gratefulness and recognition of Jesus as her teacher and Lord, becoming a faithful follower.

The Women Remain

The next time Mary Magdalene is mentioned is as a front-row participant in the events surrounding Jesus's public execution, burial, and resurrection. Her prominent role, detailed in all the Gospels, highlights her unwavering devotion to Jesus. Mary Magdalene is named by Matthew and Mark as first in the list of women at the scene of the execution, while John locates her at the foot of the cross. This strikes me as being both courageous, as the tide of public opinion at Jesus's trial had been so bloodthirsty that a riot nearly occurred, and also heartbreaking, as Mary watched her teacher, deliverer, and dear friend die a slow and agonizing death.

Mary Magdalene's prominent role highlights her unwavering devotion to Jesus.

The twelve disciples are nowhere to be found (except for John), but the women remain, looking on as Jesus's lifeless body is speared and then taken down from the cross. Mary Magdalene and Mary, Jesus's mother, watch as the body is wrapped in a cloth and laid on a stone shelf in Joseph of Arimathea's tomb. Matthew writes that the two Marys sat opposite the tomb. I'm again struck by Mary's devotion and her faithfulness. At this moment, there is no work to be done and nothing to be gained by sitting outside a sealed tomb with a dead body inside. Why did they stay with darkness approaching? Perhaps it was that their commitment to Jesus went so deep and was so strong that they were reluctant to abandon him, even when he was no longer there.

Knowing the depth of her devotion, it's no surprise, then, that Mary Magdalene is the first to return along with some of the other women. Bearing spices to anoint the body, they are stunned to find the tomb open, the body gone, and angels about. Resurrection power was in the air, and the women were not quite sure what was going on. The Gospels describe the women as first afraid, perplexed, and weeping, then joyful, trembling, and astonished as they begin to understand what had happened.

The Resurrection Encounter

The gospel of John provides the most detail about Mary Magdalene's experience at the tomb. First she sees two angels sitting on the shelf in the tomb. They ask her why she's crying, and she responds, "Because they have taken away my Lord, . . . and I don't know where they have put him" (John 20:13 NLT). Mary's devotion transcends death.

Then she hears a voice: "Dear woman, why are you crying? Who are you looking for?" I think she's crying hard by this time, unable to look up, the reality of her separation from Jesus finally sinking in. Perhaps catching a glimpse of a foot or the edge of the man's robe but not recognizing it as belonging to anyone she knows, she begs for help. "Sir, . . . if you have taken him away, tell me where you have put him, and I will go and get him" (verse 15 NLT).

Then, she recognizes the voice she loves. It's the same voice that called seven demons out of her. In shock and surprise, there's a sudden eruption of joy as she recognizes Jesus and exclaims *Rabboni*, an Aramaic word meaning "my honored teacher." It's a quiet moment between Jesus and Mary Magdalene that reflects the relationship of a tender, very committed teacher and his student or even disciple. The encounter between Mary Magdalene and Jesus ends with his charge to her to go and tell the other disciples what she had seen. Ever faithful, she does what he asked: "I have seen the Lord!" (verse 18), she proclaims to those gathered in Jerusalem mourning his loss.

In the end Mary Magdalene gave up so much; she unplugged from her home and community, sharing her money and her time. In return, she found freedom, deliverance, and an authentic relationship with her Lord that transcended death itself. Why? Because Jesus truly saw Mary and not only accepted her, but also allowed her into his inner circle. She never left, even when the threats began and violence loomed.

Mary was the *first* person to see Jesus in his resurrected body on this glorious and unprecedented day. Mary was the *first* person to touch Jesus and the *first* person to talk to Jesus. Mary was also the *first* person to be sent out with the gospel message—the good news of hope, forgiveness, and the promise of eternal life.

Mary, a woman, and one who had been demon possessed!

In John's account, Jesus approached Mary first that resurrection morning. If he hadn't, or chose not to speak to her, she likely would not have seen him and this particular story would have been very different. He was there for Mary Magdalene and he was *for* Mary Magdalene, just as he was *for* the many women in the stories of his people and his church.

Jesus saw Mary, and he sees you. He listens to you, he is for you, and he has things for you to do.

And just like Mary, we love him for it.

---

1. Have you ever experienced exclusion in a faith-based setting? What was that experience like for you? How did your body and emotions respond?
2. Is it common for you to regularly hear sermons focused on women in the Bible? Which biblical women do you want to learn more about? Which woman in Jesus's circle of disciples do you identify with most?
3. Who do you know that advocates for including women in your community? Which parts of their advocacy are most effective? How do women respond? How do men respond?

Explore: If you'd like more on Mary Magdalene, Dr. Lynn Cohick is a scholar who is interested in the lives of women, especially biblical women, in the ancient world. Her *Alabaster Jar* podcast features Mary Magdalene in episode 14, released May 2, 2024, titled "Mary Magdalene—A Model of Devotion and Discipleship."

Chapter 22

Jesus Was for the Oppressed

SARAH BUCY KLINGLER

Learn to do good;
seek justice;
rescue the oppressed;
defend the orphan;
plead for the widow.
—ISAIAH 1:17 (NRSVUE)

I was a missionary kid (MK) who spent five years during junior high and high school in the Philippines. Overall, I had a wonderful experience growing up overseas (except for the first few months, when my twelve-year-old self rebelled against leaving my friend group back home in the United States). Some of my dearest friends today are fellow MKs, which is a rare gift in today's transient world, where few people have friends that date back thirty-plus years.

Right now I have the privilege of working for MK Safety Net, a nonprofit organization that seeks to bring hope, healing, advocacy, and encouragement to adult MKs who experienced abuse while they were children on the mission field.[1] One of the reasons I'm passionate about this work is because, although my experience was quite positive, some of my peers had a much different experience. This dark side isn't something that is talked about often, if ever, because Christians tend to view missionaries with rose-colored glasses, as if they are larger-than-life spiritual giants. Putting anyone on a pedestal, though, is a dangerous thing; God alone deserves that place of honor. The truth is, there are missionaries who have abused children in ways too vile to even imagine, and many of these precious little ones who have been brave enough to disclose the evil done to them have been further oppressed by those hearing their stories. They have been slandered, shamed, and sometimes even made to feel as if the abuse were their fault. This breaks God's heart!

Jesus Sees the Unseen and Oppressed

Across every culture and generation, certain people groups—including children—have been oppressed. Right here in our own country we see it in the minimizing and cover-up of pastor pedophiles in the Southern Baptist Convention (SBC).[2] We see it in the vilification of refugees who attempt to cross the border in search of a safe haven for themselves and their children. We see it in the defending and even acceptance of high-profile celebrities who were sexual predators. While some were eventually convicted of their crimes, their money, power, and social influence allowed them to escape justice for quite some time. As is often true with powerful men, they were quickly believed and protected by far too many, while survivors were left longing for justice. It takes much time, energy, and pain for survivors to see justice, if they ever do.[3]

Oppression, according to *Collins English Dictionary*, is simply "the act of subjugating by cruelty, force, etc."[4] Let's be clear—oppression happens because people seek to gain or hold on to power. In order to gain or retain power, they don't care who or what stands in their way, so they have no problem sinning against and committing atrocious acts of evil against fellow human beings. This is completely opposite of the person and character of Jesus. In fact, when we read about his life and ministry in the Gospels, we learn of God's passion for those who are otherwise cast aside, marginalized, and even abused, particularly by people and systems of power. Jesus stood up, spoke up, and acted on behalf of the oppressed.

While all four New Testament Gospels demonstrate Jesus's concern for the oppressed, Luke in particular highlights this mission. In Luke 4, for example, we read about Jesus returning to Nazareth, the town where he grew up. On the Sabbath he goes to the synagogue and does what is customary to him—he stands up and begins to read a passage of Scripture. The passage he chooses is from the prophet Isaiah.

> The Spirit of the Lord is on me,
> because he has anointed me
> to proclaim good news to the poor.
> He has sent me to proclaim freedom for the prisoners
> and recovery of sight for the blind,
> to set the oppressed free,
> to proclaim the year of the Lord's favor.
> (Luke 4:18–19)

Not only does Jesus read these powerful words aloud, but according to verse 21 he also claims to *fulfill* these promises. This was at the start of Jesus's ministry, and it set the tone for his entire earthly mission. Jesus is indeed for the oppressed, and not only is he *for* them, but he also desires to *free* them.

Jesus stood up, spoke up, and acted on behalf of the oppressed.

Often in religious circles, whether today or in the time of Jesus, there is an insider-versus-outsider mentality. According to this mentality, if you don't believe like us, you're on the outside, and we will sometimes go to great extremes to keep you there. Somehow, Christians who embrace this mentality aim to share the liberating good news of Jesus yet do it from afar, since they don't want to be seen in proximity to "those people." Yet in Christ all boundaries were broken. He came to free all from the bondage of sin and all its ramifications, and "God's rule is established by liberating humans from 'the strong one' who holds them captive and oppresses them."[5] Forgiveness, redemption, and hope are available for all through the work of Jesus.

Jesus Reaches for the Oppressed

One of my favorite stories about Jesus's care for the marginalized is found in Luke 7:11–17. Jesus and his disciples come to the town of Nain, and as they get closer to the gate of the town, it becomes apparent they have happened upon a funeral procession. The person who had died was "the only son of his mother, and she was a widow" (verse 12). The fact that the woman who lost her son was a widow is a small yet significant piece of information. Widows were some of the most vulnerable and oppressed people in the ancient world, which operated under a patriarchal system. A woman, for the most part, was at the mercy of the men in her life (i.e., her father, husband, and sons) to care for and provide for her. Now this woman had lost not only her husband but her only son as well, and she was at risk of being impoverished or abused.

The Old Testament speaks frequently about how God's people are to care for widows, who are often mentioned alongside orphans and foreigners, because God's heart is always for the oppressed.[6] Jesus came to break down the systems of the Evil One, who loves nothing more than oppression and dehumanization. This is why in Luke 7:13 we see Jesus's heart of compassion go out to the woman who had just lost her only son. "When the Lord saw her, his heart went out to her and he said, 'Don't cry.'" I'm blown away every time I read this, and I'm challenged as well. Do I truly see people, empathize with them, and seek to help them in their desperation and time of need, like Jesus did with this widow? In my work advocating for MKs who were abused, I try to do this very thing. Sometimes simply listening to someone's story and believing them can restore hope and healing.

What happens next is a beautiful display of Jesus's liberating love and compassion. First, he touches the open stretcher where the young man's body lies. This in and of itself was an act of selfless mercy, because dead bodies were unclean according to the law. In fact, anyone who came into contact with a dead body would have been impure. (See Numbers 19:11–20 for more on this.) Even though this act fits in our minds with the Jesus we know, the original observers would have viewed it as Jesus risking impurity in order to reach out and touch the impure and bring life to the whole situation. Jesus then tells the young man to get up. And he does! Jesus, the author of life, raises him from the dead before giving him back to his mother (Luke 7:15). I get chills thinking about this woman—deep in despair and wondering how she would survive in the world alone—seeing her son come back to life. Jesus frees her from a life of oppression and gifts her with the freedom to live life to its fullest.

Jesus Calls Us to Be for the Oppressed

This is who Jesus is, which means this is also who God is. God cares about what happens to people whom others beat down, abuse, stigmatize, and turn away from, and if we claim to be his followers, we must care also. Too often we're so overly concerned with people's spiritual standing that we forget about their physical needs. Too often "our preaching, so concerned about the beyond, frequently runs the risk of having little to say to those who must still live amidst the injustice and suffering of the present."[7] Our faith is an embodied faith, and we carry the good news with us in both word and deed. In a world where power, wealth, and social standing are so important, Jesus comes to subvert these values and to demonstrate the worth and value of all.

This is the reality of his upside-down kingdom to come "on earth as it is in heaven" (Matthew 6:10).

The challenge today is the same as it was then. Are we willing to risk our own reputation, our own "cleanness," even our comfortable lifestyles to lift up the oppressed? Jesus healed, blessed, spoke words of comfort over, forgave the sins of, and invited to the table the oppressed of his time—women, children, tax collectors, the demon possessed, lepers, Samaritans, and sinners. If this feels like an overwhelming task to you, remember Jesus's words in Matthew 25:36, 40: "I needed clothes and you clothed me, I was sick and you looked after me, I was in prison and you came to visit me. . . . Truly I tell you, whatever you did for one of the least of these brothers and sisters of mine, you did for me." Small acts of kindness and mercy demonstrate care to those who are oppressed. Listen to their stories. Weep with them. Eat with them. Help meet their physical needs. Find ways to lift them up. And, of course, always point them to Jesus.

> Lord Jesus, we thank you that you are no respecter of persons. You came to this earth in a humble way, as a vulnerable baby nestled in a lowly manger, and spent the early years of your life as a refugee. You know what it means to be oppressed, and your earthly ministry demonstrates your love for oppressed peoples. Give us your heart, Jesus. Open our eyes to people's needs. May we point people to the hope you give for both spiritual and physical restoration. Thank you for opening your arms to embrace all who would call upon your name. Thank you that you are a God who is for the oppressed. Amen.

---

1. Think about your local community. Who around you faces oppression? What systems or social beliefs keep certain people in

vulnerable positions? Have you experienced oppression in your own community?

2. How do your body and emotions respond to Jesus announcing his mission as proclaiming good news to the poor, freedom for the prisoners, sight for the blind, and freedom for the oppressed? Do you identify with any of these groups of people?
3. Who do you know that models action on behalf of oppressed people?

Explore: Find a group in your local community that advocates for an oppressed group in your midst. Learn the key points of advocacy for this group and make a donation or spend time working or volunteering on their behalf.

Chapter 23

Jesus Was Loving to His Enemies

LEO DIAZ

You have heard that it was said, "Love your neighbor and hate your enemy." But I tell you, love your enemies and pray for those who persecute you, that you may be children of your Father in heaven.

—Matthew 5:43–45

Before a packed conference hall, I watched as an elderly man emptied himself of many years' worth of tears as he relived the trauma he endured in his homeland. This gentleman told us about how he immigrated to the United States in the early sixties following Castro's takeover of the onetime *Perla del Caribe* (Pearl of the Caribbean). The roundtable was created by a local nonprofit to raise awareness for the mental health of political refugees.

I was moved watching this man share his dramatic story of exile and the savagery of the Castro regime toward the innocent people of Cuba. I witnessed him weep as he recalled the brutal assault and eventual death of his older brother during a home invasion by Castro's police force. He went on to share with vivid detail the events that followed that tragic moment and all that led to their escape from their beloved Cuba. Without question, the one common theme in all his recollections was Castro. As the segment concluded, one of the panelists, having noticed him referring to the now deceased dictator as "that man" throughout his address, asked him if he was willing to share some final thoughts about Castro, to which he replied sharply, "I have learned to subdue my hatred for him over the years."

I can relate to the story and emotions this man shared that evening and his reluctance to utter the name that had brought him and his family so much pain. I am a first-generation Cuban American, and Fidel Castro was a recurring topic of discussion around the dinner table growing up. When he died in 2016, many in my family, myself included, joined exiled Cubans from around the world to celebrate as their longtime adversary had finally met his fate. For people who have lived under oppressive regimes, celebrating the death of the oppressor seems not only natural but appropriate. One could even say that the historically oppressed are entitled to despise their enemy, to hate the one who has subjugated and dehumanized them. Yet it is against this framework that Jesus presents to his first-century followers one of his most controversial ethics—love for the enemy.

Jesus's Rebranded Teaching on Love

It's easy to love people who are easy to love. And chances are, the people we find the easiest to love are those we click with on a personal level—people who look like us or think like us or vote like us. Naturally, we are extra kind to those we relate with. In many regards, it is considerably easier to pray for those who love us back. We are comfortable with our world intersecting with theirs. Although loving those we are familiar with isn't inherently wrong, it falls short of the brand of love that Jesus inaugurated in the Gospels. In what has famously been titled the Sermon on the Plain (Luke 6:20–49), Jesus asserts that loving and doing good to those who love us are common among all people groups and therefore unworthy of any special credit (verses 32–34). He follows this with a shocking directive to love our enemies (verses 35–36). Unbeknownst to those in attendance, Jesus was rewriting the book on love. For him, loving people who are naturally difficult to love would be the distinguishing mark of members of God's new-creation family.

This kingdom motif of virtuous, barrier-breaking enemy love represents the backdrop for Luke's Sermon on the Plain. With a little context we realize that Jesus was surrounded by people who would not have taken well to this subversive message. To grasp the significance of what Jesus did here, we need to get a feel for the atmosphere of the scene. First, Jesus delivered this rebranded teaching on love after a series of blatant Sabbath-breaking exploits: reaping grain heads from a field and healing a disabled man after crashing a synagogue service in full view of scribes and Pharisees (Luke 6:1–11), the same fellows who promulgated the observance of the ancient Jewish laws. One can suspect that as a result of this seemingly defiant behavior, discussions about Jesus and his motley crew of followers circulated among the religious insiders. Undoubtedly, conversations about halting the momentum of this new movement spread. So, over the course of Jesus's time on earth, he gained not only a good number of followers but also a sizable group of enemies.

Loving people who are naturally difficult to love would be the distinguishing mark of God's new-creation family.

To drive home the weight of this defining moment in Jesus's kingdom tour, Luke tells us Jesus was surrounded by "a large crowd of his disciples . . . and a great number of people from all over Judea, from Jerusalem, and from the coastal region around Tyre and Sidon" (verse 17). The setting Luke paints for us is composed of Jews from Judea and Jerusalem, and Phoenicians from Tyre and Sidon. To a first-century observer, the irony would have been difficult to overlook. There on a level plain, Jesus delivers a revolutionary message about enemy love before a crowd of natural-born enemies. Years of political and economic differences between Jews and Phoenicians could not prevent them from gathering together to listen to Messiah Jesus. Nor could it keep an anti-Roman revolutionary like Simon the Zealot from coexisting with Matthew, a tax collector on Roman payroll, as disciples of Jesus. The scene that Luke depicts for us consists of people of different cultures, theological worldviews, and political allegiances. Groups who normally would not dare breathe the same air. Groups who in those times were said to be "incompatible." Yet there they were, outsiders rubbing elbows with insiders, the historically oppressed sharing space with the oppressor. All of them breathing the same air while a mysterious Galilean urged them to "love your enemies, do good to those who hate you" (verse 27)—in other words, love the one you might be standing right next to. Adding to the marvel of this message, Jesus delivered it while his own enemies multiplied and plotted his arrest and eventual murder.

In Matthew's parallel to Luke's Sermon on the Plain, Jesus reminds his audience that the Father "causes his sun to rise on the evil and the good, and sends rain on the righteous and the unrighteous" (Matthew 5:45). The correlation that Jesus draws between the impartiality of the sun and rain and the Father's love toward the good and the evil, the friend and the enemy, could not be made any clearer. God's love stretches beyond conventional stereotypes, bending social protocols to demonstrate his indiscriminate goodness and love to every human, especially those we have historically despised.

A Demonstration of Love

This new ethic of love that Jesus embedded into the social order was not left to mere words; rather, they were embodied by him, evidenced later in Matthew when Jesus is said to be a "friend of tax collectors and sinners" (11:19). On the cross, Jesus prayed for the ones who plotted his death (Luke 23:34), incarnating the words he spoke that day on the plain before a crowd of enemies. There is, however, an important distinction that must be made when we consider Jesus's directive to love our enemies.

For good reason, *agape* is the Greek word used for love in this context as opposed to the terms *philia* (the word Greeks used to describe friendship) or *eros* (a fiery word that represented sexual desire). *Agape* is a radical term rarely used in the first century that describes the choice, however difficult, to will the highest good for all humans—friend or foe.[1] This is a stunning redefinition of love that is used to make a clear distinction in how followers of Jesus are to love others regardless of who the recipient is. Even knowing how deeply embedded the wound of the enemy might be in all of us, Jesus tells us to love by way of willing goodness toward those we naturally despise. He said, "Bless those who curse you, pray for those who mistreat you" (Luke 6:28). Jesus shows us that indiscriminate love and prayer are the DNA of the kingdom of God.

Years have passed since that roundtable, but the trembling words of that man—"I have learned to subdue my hatred"—have stayed with me. I think about what it means to subdue hate without erasing history. I think about my own family—the years of unresolved trauma, the fiery conversations about Castro growing up, and that day in 2016 when diaspora Cubans everywhere celebrated his death. But I also think about Jesus, standing on that plain and commanding us to love our enemies, not because they deserve it, but because hatred begets hatred—the very thing Jesus came to set us free from.

Since committing to Jesus's love ethic, I've learned that loving our enemies does not mean ignoring the past and overlooking injustice. It means choosing a future that is marked not by vengeance but by a love that holds mercy and justice in the same breath. Like that man at the roundtable, we might choose to never speak the name of those who hurt us, but by learning to subdue hatred for them and desiring that

God's goodness find its way to them, we might reclaim a part of us we thought we had lost.

---

1. We all experience different levels of hurt. Could you identify with the man's emotions in the opening story? In what ways does sharing a story like this affect both the one sharing and the community hearing it?
2. Who do you know that is good at loving their enemies? Do they use unconventional means to show love to people who oppose them? Have you experienced love from someone you considered an enemy?
3. Who are the bitterly opposed groups in your local community? What might it look like for them to begin to love each other? Does one group have more social power or wealth than another? Does that advantage affect what love looks like between opposing groups?

Explore: Reflect on how your body feels and what emotions you experience when you hear stories of oppression and/or forgiveness.

Chapter 24

Jesus Was a Servant

SCOTT JOHANNINGSMEIER

For even the Son of Man did not come to be served, but to serve.

—Mark 10:45

I was very fortunate to know all my grandparents, and I have learned something from each one of them. One of my grandfathers taught me what a servant was. He was the town handyman and loved working on his neighbors' houses. At his funeral we reflected on how he probably worked on every house in his small town. He didn't do it to become rich, because he wasn't. He did it because he had the knowledge and the ability to help, and his neighbors and friends had needs. Grandpa served others. He was a true servant shaped after Jesus.

The Christ Hymn of Philippians 2:6–11 reveals how the early church understood Jesus. The hymn opens by acknowledging Jesus as being in very nature God (verse 6). This means that every attribute, characteristic, and power that is found in God is also found in Jesus. He was the true representation of God on earth and had every right to claim this identity. However, the hymn takes a turn and proclaims Jesus as not considering his equality with God as something to be used for his advantage. Jesus did not consider his status and power as something to be used for his own good but rather in service to others.

Instead of lifting himself up to a position worthy of his status, Jesus took on the very nature of a servant (verse 7). When you speak of someone's nature, you are discussing who they are at their core. Jesus, at his core, was God. However, he did not just pretend to be a servant or temporarily assume the role of a servant. In his very nature Jesus became a servant. The truth of Jesus as a servant is found through his words and actions.

Servanthood over Status

Matthew 20:20–28 is an example of Jesus not encouraging status and power but emphasizing servanthood. The mother of two of the disciples asks Jesus to let her sons sit in the places of honor when his kingdom is fulfilled. His answer to the request is to tell them they do not know what they are asking (verse 22). Of course, the other disciples hear about the request and become upset with the two disciples. The jockeying for position among the disciples has begun, so Jesus calls the disciples together. Jesus uses this moment to explain to the disciples the difference between the power and privilege of the world and the nature of a servant in God's kingdom. "You know that the rulers of the Gentiles lord it over them, and their high officials exercise authority over them. Not so with you. Instead, whoever wants to become great among you must be your servant, and whoever wants to be first must be your slave—just as the Son of Man did not come to be served, but to serve, and to give his life as a ransom for many" (verses 25–28).

The issue at hand, as demonstrated in the request from the mother of these disciples, is of status, power, and privilege. How do we obtain status so it will work for our advantage? Jesus addresses this issue head-on by reminding the disciples how the rulers of this world use their positions of power to benefit themselves. Those who have status and power use others, especially servants and slaves, to build and keep their power. The servants are below their masters, and the powerful consider status as something to be used for their own advantage.

As the one who did not consider his nature as God something to be used for his own advantage, Jesus tells the disciples the way of the world is not to be the way for them. Anyone wanting to be considered great must serve others. The ultimate example of someone of great power serving others is Jesus himself, who came not to be served but to serve. This is who Jesus was because the nature of God is to have the nature of a servant.

Serving Through Strength

Think about the people you know who have the attitude of a servant. You probably would say they are willing to help anyone. Typically, we see them using their gifts and strengths for others. Throughout the Bible God is seen as a helper for Israel. For example, Psalm 146 praises God's nature as a helper as being the ultimate source of hope for the Israelites. The powerful people of the world are no help to Israel because they do not have true power; God is the one with the true power. He has the ability to provide for Israel's needs, and therefore he does.

> Don't put your confidence in powerful people;
>   there is no help for you there.
> When they breathe their last, they return to the earth,
>   and all their plans die with them.
> But joyful are those who have the God of Israel as their *helper*,
>   whose hope is in the Lord their God.
>
> (verses 3–5 NLT)

The true beauty of Psalm 146 rests not in God's role as Israel's source of help. It is in how God helps. A servant in the Bible does not help to accomplish the goals or aspirations of a master. The nature of a biblical servant is to provide for those in need. In its entirety, Psalm 146 details exactly how God helps Israel. He gives justice to the oppressed. He feeds the hungry and frees prisoners. He heals the blind and removes the burdens from the weary. He protects foreigners, orphans, and widows. This is what a biblical servant does, and Jesus understood this as part of his purpose. At the beginning of his ministry, he went into the synagogue and read from Isaiah, saying he had come to proclaim good news to the poor, free prisoners, heal the blind, and free the oppressed (Luke 4:18–19).

Jesus Demonstrates Serving Others

A servant will help from their strength. In John 13, Jesus brings his actions and teaching together to demonstrate what it means to humble oneself and take on the nature of a servant. In this chapter, Jesus gathers with his disciples to celebrate Passover, a gathering we today refer to as the "Last Supper," since it was held on the night when Jesus was arrested. John tells us Jesus knew what was to come. He knew the plans of Judas to betray him. Despite this, Jesus still served others in his final meal with his disciples.

The nature of a biblical servant is to provide for those in need.

Jesus's nature as God and as a servant was on full display during this final evening together with his disciples. John 13:3 says, "Jesus knew that the Father had given him authority over everything and that he had come from God and would return to God" (NLT). What a powerful statement concerning the nature of God in Jesus. To have authority over everything is what the powerful people of the world want. Yet, in this moment before he was betrayed, Jesus chose not to use his power to serve himself. What he did was surprising. "So he got up from the table, took off his robe, wrapped a towel around his waist, and poured water into a basin. Then he began to wash the disciples' feet, drying them with the towel he had around him" (verses 4–5 NLT). Jesus's understanding of the relationship between power and servanthood could not be clearer than in these three verses. Jesus had all authority to change what was about to happen, so he stripped down like a servant and washed feet. Because of his power and not in spite of it, Jesus becomes like a servant in dress and deed. Even when Peter protests that Jesus should never wash his feet, Jesus still serves his disciples, telling Peter, "You don't understand now what I am doing, but someday you will" (verse 7 NLT). The power of God is found in the nature of a servant.

The selfless nature of Jesus's servanthood is further revealed when we realize that among those whom Jesus washed was Judas. Jesus knew that Judas would betray him that night and yet he still washed Judas's feet. In doing so, Jesus exemplifies that the nature of a servant is not to serve those who are worthy of being served. It is to serve everyone regardless of their deeds. The ones whom the world says are not worthy to be served are the ones that Jesus, in his power, served.

Would I serve Judas?

Would you?

John says next that after Jesus washes the feet of the disciples, he taught them about becoming a servant. He was their teacher. He was their Lord. He gave them the example to follow; they must humble themselves and put the needs of others ahead of themselves. This is the nature of a godly servant: "Do as I have done to you" (verse 15 NLT).

It was the servant nature of Jesus that shaped my grandfather's life. He learned from Jesus what it means to use your strength and abilities to help others. He learned what it means to humble yourself and do the dirty work. He learned to serve those with the greatest needs. And last but not least, he learned to encourage others to do the same, which is what I learned from him.

Every day I pray that I may have the same impact on my children by showing what it means to be a servant like Jesus was. There was an elderly man who lived next to us for fifteen years. Whenever it would snow, even though most of the time it was just a light dusting, I would take my children to shovel his drive and walkway. We didn't do it for money, and we turned him down every time he offered to pay us. We worked out in the cold because our neighbor had a need, and we had the ability to help. We shoveled driveways just as Jesus washed feet, so my children and I could show our neighbor the love of God through our service.

---

1. What characteristics influence a person's social status in your local community? In what ways are these characteristics the same and/or different from how God values people?
2. Who in your life models serving those in need? How does your community respond to their service? Do others join in?
3. The breadth of community needs can be overwhelming. How do you decide what needs to help with? Have you ever served the needs of others when you weren't particularly skilled in that area? What does it look like to serve from your strength?

Explore: Write out a list of ways you are skilled to help with needs in your local community. Is there an individual or organization that could use your skills?

Chapter 25

Jesus Was Nonpolitical

TYLER CALLAHAN

"You are a king, then!" said Pilate.
Jesus answered, "You say that I am a king. In fact, the reason
I was born and came into the world is to testify to the truth.
Everyone on the side of truth listens to me."
—John 18:37

I was born near the tail end of the denim-clad summer of 1995, which made the infamous 2016 election the first I was eligible to vote in. *What an introduction to American democracy.* But as the dust of the campaign trail swirled and the mudslinging began, I found myself not in Indiana with the rest of my peers but in England with a unique opportunity to experience the tension of that season as both a citizen *and* a spectator. I remember calling my dad one night in an anxious fog, asking questions like "Are the candidates always this rude?" and "Are people always this intense?" He wasn't sure how to answer.

Before the 2016 election, my only engagement with politics was an AP government class my junior year of high school. I took an online test for one of my assignments, and it told me I was 51 percent Republican, 49 percent Democrat, and 100 percent confused as to what any of that meant. As a polite Midwestern pastor's kid, I knew just enough about politics to stay out of it, choosing instead to focus on "spiritual things." So, if you were to tell seventeen-year-old me, "Jesus was nonpolitical," I wouldn't have batted an eye. But it's not that simple, is it?

The truth is that, in one sense, Jesus was *overtly* political. His prophetic way of life and his gospel message were deeply concerned with power relations, especially as they related to the distribution of resources. You don't need to look long to find a quote from Jesus about feeding the hungry or supporting the poor (Matthew 25:34–40). You'd more easily thread a camel through the eye of a needle than read the Gospels without noticing Jesus's concern for the "least of these" (verse 40). Depending on which gospel account you read, you might even say that the distribution of resources (time, money, energy, etc.) and the empowerment of the disempowered were Jesus's *primary* concerns while on earth. For instance, Jesus's mission from Luke's perspective is most clearly summarized in his quotation of Isaiah in Luke 4:18–19:

> The Spirit of the Lord is on me,
> because he has anointed me
> to proclaim good news to the poor.
> He has sent me to proclaim freedom for the prisoners
> and recovery of sight for the blind,
> to set the oppressed free,
> to proclaim the year of the Lord's favor.

In another sense, though, we see example after example of Jesus *distancing* himself from the political systems and structures that we assume are vital to accomplishing that mission today. Take, for instance, Jesus's temptation in the wilderness. In Matthew 4:8–9, Satan takes Jesus to a high mountain to show him "all the kingdoms of the world and their splendor" (verse 8). "All this I will give you," the tempter says, but Jesus refuses (verse 9). And he didn't refuse this offer only from the Father of Lies. In John 6 after the feeding of the five thousand, we read that "Jesus, knowing that they intended to come and make him king by force, withdrew again to a mountain by himself" (verse 15). Jesus wasn't interested in worldly power, status, or office (John 18:36). Rather, he spent time around people he knew could hurt his reputation. In a Greco-Roman culture that was oriented to honor and shame as social currency, and within a religious tradition that placed strict boundaries around the clean and unclean, Jesus spent most of his time associating with those the Pharisees called "sinners" (Mark 2:16).

To take it a step further, one of Jesus's most direct statements about the nature of political allegiance seems deliberately to separate the *religious* and the *political*. In Matthew 22 we see the Pharisees trying to "trap [Jesus] in his words" (verse 15), so they send their disciples to ask him a loaded question: "Is it right to pay the imperial tax to Caesar or not?" (verse 17). Jesus's response is characteristically smart, but it is also commonly misinterpreted (or at least overemphasized):

> But Jesus, knowing their evil intent, said, "You hypocrites, why are you trying to trap me? Show me the coin used for paying the tax." They brought him a denarius, and he asked them, "Whose image is this? And whose inscription?"
>
> "Caesar's," they replied.
>
> Then he said to them, "*So give back to Caesar what is Caesar's, and to God what is God's.*" (verses 18–21)

Jesus's charge to "give back to Caesar what is Caesar's" has often been misapplied (and occasionally abused) in much the same way as Paul's instruction to submit to authorities in Romans 13. That is to say that people who *already* have power and privilege have tended to use these statements to manipulate those below them into maintaining and supporting that power. *But that's not what Jesus was saying.* Rather, Jesus is laying out his revolutionary political ideology—his way of understanding how power and resources should ultimately be distributed. Put simply: *The church is the politics of Jesus.*[1]

Politics, Power, and Resources

Among the myriad disagreements between the political Left and Right in America is the clash between the ideals of "big government" and "small government." If you can forgive a bit of an oversimplification, it could be said that the argument is really about *power over resources.* Should the government be trusted to oversee the distribution of resources, or should individuals have the power to determine how to use what they have? In Jesus and in the early church, along with his closest disciples and friends, we find a third way. Consider the passage from Matthew 22 mentioned earlier. When we quote these verses in our discussions about power over resources, we often short-change Jesus's sentiment. We acknowledge Jesus's concession to "give to Caesar what is Caesar's," but we often neglect to consider his command to give "to God what is God's." It's clear from the surrounding verses what belongs to Caesar: taxes. But what belongs to God?

We were created and are now redeemed because God, who is Love (1 John 4:16), loves us (Romans 5:8). The only fitting response to that kind of love is to give it back to God by giving it away to others (1 John 4:19–20). This self-giving impulse applies to our motivations and relationships, as well as to how we use our power and resources. For example, in the book of Acts we see the early church engage in a radical form of resource sharing, holding everything "in common" (2:44). While this was the result of a move of the Spirit, which required willingness on behalf of the individuals, the collection and distribution itself was ultimately organized and overseen by the apostles (4:34–35). This is what is meant by "The church is the politics of Jesus." Jesus's teachings on what we should do with what we have are clear: Give it away to those in need (Matthew 19:16–24). But who should be trusted to oversee it all—the government or the individual? Neither. Instead, the people of God are called to embody self-giving, power-divesting love in the world *as a community*.

Jesus Embodies a Different Power

As we can see, Jesus's politics are of a completely different nature than ours. Especially in America (though I presume this to be true for much of the West), the word *political* has become shorthand for partisan bickering, desperate grasps at domination, and extremist allegiance to a set of ideas typically originating from whichever media outlet can best appeal to our unconscious fears and biases. If this is what we mean, then Jesus could not be further from political. Instead, Christ embodies a sort of power that in every way counters the Western political ideal by relinquishing his control and relegating his divinity to identify with those who have no money, no status, no contacts, and no influence to impart. It is the power of self-giving love.

The people of God are called to embody self-giving, power-divesting love.

For people who long to become more like Jesus, this has massive implications for the ways we engage with politics. We're called to reject any ideologies that might co-opt the name of Jesus for the sake of the political upper hand, regardless of how noble the cause. *Jesus is not a mascot for a political party.* He is our King, and we are citizens of *his* kingdom. And as citizens of that heavenly kingdom, we're compelled not to hitch our wagons to parties or figures who promise to smooth our path to worldly power. Instead, we're called to be ambassadors of the upside-down kingdom of God in the here and now, a kingdom in which power and status are flipped on their heads. The last are first; the first are last (Matthew 20:16). The poor and needy are blessed (Luke 6:20). The hungry are filled with good things, and the rich are sent away empty (1:53).

I've learned much since the election of 2016, both about the broken, power-grabbing politics in our country and about my own temptation to participate in those politics. I've learned that most issues are far less cut and dried than we'd like them to be. I've learned that on the other end of any given political ideology, there is a person who bears God's image. Most of all, I've learned that to be an ambassador of God's kingdom in a country that seems to be growing more divided with each election cycle, we must reject the power dynamics of the world around us and seek first the justice, wholeness, and generosity that accompanies Jesus's reign, regardless of the social, economic, or "political" consequences. We must prefer *love* over leverage; we must love *people* more than power. Only then will we be able to be engaged citizens, voters, campaigners, and contributors to our society who fully represent the heart of God to and for all creation.

---

1. Do you engage in political discussions? How do your body and emotions respond when you hear about current political issues?
2. Did you grow up in a faith community that saw Jesus as overtly political (concerned about power relations and the distribution of resources) or as separated from political allegiance (distanced from political systems and structures)? How do you respond to the quote, "The church is the politics of Jesus"?
3. How does partisan allegiance and desire for domination affect your local community? Where do you see people separate based on political allegiance? How does this separation affect your community?

Explore: Spend time (perhaps a month or more) repeatedly reading through or listening to one of the New Testament Gospels. Make notes when you notice Jesus's concerns about power relations and the distribution of resources as well as his distance from political systems and structures. Reflect on how these intersect with your local community.

Chapter 26

Jesus Was Forgiving

TERRI FULLERTON

And forgive us our debts,
as we also have forgiven our debtors.
—Matthew 6:12

There was a long stretch many years ago when these seven words, "as we also have forgiven our debtors," got stuck in my throat, and I swallowed hard at this part of the Lord's Prayer rather than praying it. Intimate acts of betrayal had left me with deep, flinching wounds. I didn't know how to forgive what had brought so many unwanted consequences. I vacillated between anger, sadness, and shame.

How could reciting this prayer turn forgiveness into *past* tense? As if it had already happened? Forgiveness—was it even possible?!

In the 1990s, the evangelical church taught that feelings get in the way of forgiveness, so I concluded I shouldn't *have* feelings because they weren't trustworthy. This unbiblical lens leads to a disembodied theology where separating yourself from your feelings is the answer, adding heavy rocks to an already full backpack for someone on a steep uphill climb. Moreover, forgiveness is used to silence people, avoiding honesty to hide what is dysfunctional, toxic, or even evil. Teaching forgiveness at the expense of truth is like giving plastic fruit to people who are starving. It's deceptive and neglects the messy process.

Forgiveness is also difficult because we receive mixed messages on what it even means.

Sorting Out Forgiveness

In his book *The Art of Forgiving*, Lewis Smedes shares that when most people say they can't forgive, they also have a misconception about what it means. Forgiveness does not mean the wounds inflicted on you are okay or that you need to tolerate them. Smedes emphasizes that we do not diminish the wrongness of what was done to us.[1] For example, Jesus doesn't ever say forgiveness means forgetting the harm that occurred. God gave us memory, and it's a gift. I thought when I left home that the best thing to do was bury the pain. But buried pain and segmented feelings don't lead to healing. Painful memories can become healed memories through therapy and forgiveness.

Forgiveness is not the same as reconciliation. Reconciliation is between two people and often involves forgiveness, especially with a friend or family member. However, some people are harmful, and it's not wise to reunite with that spouse, friend, or offender. It also may mean that you never are alone with that person again.

Forgiveness is for the mind and heart of the one deeply harmed. It isn't necessarily felt from the heart. The choice to forgive releases the power an offender may hold over you. As you participate in practicing forgiveness, you realize it is a gift for the one who has been deeply wounded so that bitterness doesn't take root. Forgiveness does not mean that the wounds inflicted on you are okay or that you need to continue to tolerate abuse or violence. It doesn't mean sweeping the truth under the rug. You can forgive someone without having a discussion with an unsafe person. There may never be an apology.

Examples of Forgiveness

Forgiveness does not dismiss consequences. Rachel Denhollander publicly forgave the physician who molested her and many other gymnasts.

I can imagine how difficult it was to do so, but I know it didn't come as public disregard of what happened. Some of her fellow Olympic teammates gave testimonies as well.[2]

Following the mass shooting in 2015 in Charleston, South Carolina, at Mother Emanuel AME Church, Felicia Sanders, who lost her son, and Nadine Collier, who lost her mother, offered forgiveness to Dylann Roof at his hearing.[3] Forgiveness does not remove consequences in a culture that pursues truth and justice. This is evident in the identity of Jesus.

In my journey, I knew I needed to wrestle with this difficult teaching. I saw how bitterness became deeply rooted in the hearts of some family members in multiple generations. As a parent I wanted to break the cycle. I read Desmond Tutu's book *No Future Without Forgiveness* and learned how the South African Truth and Reconciliation Committee honored the traumatic stories of apartheid in that country.[4] Through this organization, the victims of apartheid embodied the pain it caused as they recounted murders, rape, and widespread systemic evil in front of some of those who perpetrated the evil. They didn't bypass truth and justice in seeking healing. I personally learned from Tutu's book how vital forgiveness is to healing.

Following the Spirit's Guidance

As I thought about what helped me find some footing in this journey of forgiveness, I recalled times at Target when our children were three and five years old. Like many children at that age, they bounced with excitement at helping to push the cart. I knew as a teacher and mother that letting young children "help" can be more time consuming than just doing it yourself but nevertheless is valuable. They would put their little fingers through the holes of the carts and push, though without my help they would have run into people and merchandise. Because I wanted to get down an aisle and not grow old before reaching the checkout, I pushed the cart to guide them. Of course, as the cart became heavier, they needed my strength to push the weight. They were willing, but they weren't quite strong enough. I delighted in their desire and thanked them for their "help."

The Spirit impressed on me one time that this image is where to start with forgiveness: a desire to be willing to stay in step with Jesus. So I pushed through and trusted God to work in my heart and carry the weight. I started praying out loud in the car when I was alone. I admitted that I didn't feel forgiving but I choose to forgive ______ for _______. How many times did I need to do this? God and I are *continually* pushing this cart together. Forgiveness, I've learned, is a step that becomes a discipline; it is not a final, cathartic resolution.

Jesus and Forgiveness

Forgiveness was at the heart of Jesus's mission. Forgiving others is the very core of why he came and what he did for those of us in the margins, the sick, poor, and hungry. Out of his vast love God came to dwell among the people and declare their sins were forgiven. Jesus invited others to join him as he brought this new way of living to our world. God wanted to break the cycle of sin that betrays, oppresses, abuses, and repeats itself. What stops the cycle of fracturing is forgiveness. It's a hard teaching and Jesus knows this. He even teaches us to pray for this daily. As followers, God wants us to imitate his words and actions to show another way to a weary world that longs for more than fighting, division, and hatred.

Forgiveness is a step that becomes a discipline.

This is the ultimate gift to us. Jesus died for us to forgive our sins and deal with the fracturing of sin that separated us from God. In his hardest hour on the cross after betrayal, abandonment, a false mob with unjust accusations, and flogging, Jesus carried the wooden beams that would lead to his crucifixion. In his most painful last hours, he asked his Father to forgive them. Those who inflicted the physical and emotional wounds were not sorry. Those who carried out the trials didn't apologize and admit their wrongdoing. Those who mocked him and plotted evil against him were not brokenhearted.

Out of his extravagant mercy he showed his disciples how to move forward without bitterness or retaliation. Jesus even taught us, his disciples, to pray daily to our Father, seeking his will and goodness to spread throughout our communities so that they will flourish (Matthew 6:9–13). He knew that such restorative work would take forgiveness rooted in grace. He knew we need to orient ourselves daily to form the discipline of forgiveness, so he included it in the Lord's Prayer: "Forgive us our debts, as we have also forgiven our debtors" (verse 12).

A Story About Forgiveness and Unforgiveness

In Matthew 18:23–35 Jesus tells a parable about what forgiveness looks like for his followers. It's like a king who wants to settle debts with his servants who owe him money. One man owed ten thousand talents, an amount of money equivalent to almost a thousand years of wages. Since the servant couldn't pay it, the master asks him to sell everything he and his family owns. The servant falls to his knees and begs him to be patient and promises he will surely pay him back. The master has pity on him, cancels the entire debt, and lets him go rather than putting him in prison, where he would never be able to pay down his debt.

Released from debt, the man goes free and sees one of his workers who owes him one hundred denarii, an amount equivalent to a few months of labor. He grabs the servant and chokes him, demanding that he get his money back. His servant falls to his knees and begs him to be patient, promising he will pay all he owes him. But instead of giving him mercy he has his servant thrown in prison, where he can't pay off his debt. When the other servants hear what happened, they become livid and tell the master. The master summons the servant who refused to be patient with his fellow servant. He calls him a "wicked servant" and reminds him how he compassionately canceled the outrageous debt that he would never be able to repay, exclaiming, "Shouldn't you have had mercy on your fellow servant as I had on you?" He hands him over to the prison guards to be tortured in prison until he pays off his debt.

Jesus says that this is how it will be for you and me if we don't forgive our brothers and sisters from the heart. When people receive the unmerited gift of God's forgiveness, it transforms hearts. This parable is about a person who has received this forgiveness by being released from a debt they couldn't pay back in a thousand years, which is all of us. It's also a story about what happens when we don't forgive. A lack of mercy grows something in us that Jesus knows will create havoc. A lack of forgiveness births bitterness and imprisons us. It eats away at the good in us and keeps us from flourishing.

This is a hard teaching. Jesus wants us to participate in this new way of life together, on earth as it is in heaven. Concerning this new humanity, Jesus tells us how we can be life-giving people who love others well so that they may see the heart of God. As we yield again and again to the act of forgiveness, we inch, oh so slowly, toward making forgiveness a past tense action. There's blessed mercy and grace in that word after those last three letters are dropped and it becomes *forgiven*, our prayer and our resting place.

---

1. How were you taught the meaning of forgiveness? Have you needed to modify your understanding over the years? What prompted your understanding to change or stay the same?
2. Do you have an image or metaphor, like the example of the author's children pushing the cart with her in Target, that helps

you understand and practice forgiveness? How does revisiting this image shape you?

3. Who can you talk with about this "hard teaching" from Jesus? What resources does your faith community offer for understanding how to follow Jesus in forgiveness?

Explore: Read the book *The Art of Forgiving* by Lewis Smedes or *No Future Without Forgiveness* by Desmond Tutu. Listen to "What Forgiveness Is and Isn't (The Lord's Prayer Pt. 4)" by the *Bible Project* podcast (episode 415). What insights did you learn about the practice of forgiveness from these resources? How do they reshape your understanding?

Chapter 27

Jesus Was Prayerful

BETHANY HAMMER

But Jesus often withdrew to lonely places and prayed.
—LUKE 5:16

When my head hit my pillow, I couldn't control my tears. My eighteen-year-old self finally gave in to a moment of deep grief for my mother's unexpected death. It was not fair. I did not get to say goodbye. I prayed harder in the darkness of my bedroom that evening than I had ever prayed before. My eyes focused on one spot at the bottom right end of my bed while I earnestly pleaded with God to just let me see her once more.

There were so many people that God surrounded my family with during that difficult time, people who prayed for us and walked with us. I had so many conversations that they all became somewhat of a blur, but one statement in particular transformed my prayer life: "It is okay to yell and scream at God. God already knows how you are feeling—the sorrow and emotions you are going through are not a surprise to him." Up until that point, I had never felt permitted to talk with God so honestly and informally. I was always taught that God is a holy God whom we should come to in a posture of respect, not a God to whom you could "yell and scream." However, when you look at the life of Jesus, you can see what an authentic prayer life looks like.

Each of the Gospels portrays prayer somewhat differently, but all of them draw attention to Jesus's intimacy with the Father. Jesus, who was fully human and fully divine, experienced the pain of this sinful world. He went to God in all circumstances—healing for the sick, perseverance, empowerment, assurances, divine guidance, and more. It is impossible to focus on all of it here. However, the Gospels portray Jesus's prayer life as critical for the mission God had set before him. We can discover three main characteristics of a prayerful life when looking at Jesus's time in prayer on the Mount of Olives before his crucifixion (Luke 22)—his authenticity, his desires, and God's response.

Authenticity

To begin, Jesus prayed to God authentically. God is not a God who only wants you to go to him with formality; he does not require every prayer to undergo the formalities of heads bowed, eyes closed, knees down, and hands folded. He desires our complete, embodied, and emotional labor of prayer—earnest prayer that produces sweat "like great drops of blood" (verse 44 NRSVue). According to Paul, when we do not know how to pray, God promises us the "Spirit intercedes with groanings too deep for words" (Romans 8:26 NRSVue). Jesus went into his time of prayer on the Mount of Olives in *agony*. The word used in Greek communicates someone who is *fearfully* fighting a battle. Jesus does not just check in with God every now and again or go to him solely when he needs something. Jesus's time in prayer with his Father is a time of emotional honesty.[1] Jesus does not hide his fear, and God is not surprised by Jesus's fear. Your prayers do not surprise God. He is not shocked that you are angry, fearful, confused, or in pain. Just as Jesus went to God in his time of agony, you too can go to God in all times and be authentic about what you are experiencing, and when you have no words, the groans of the Spirit will intercede for you. It is this exact intimate conversation with God that reveals a genuine relationship between you and him, just as it did for Jesus himself.[2]

Desires

Second, Jesus prayed to God for his desires: "Remove this cup from me" (Luke 22:42 NRSVUE). Jesus knew his purpose in his earthly mission was for the salvation of all people. He understood and accepted this. However, on the Mount of Olives he came to God earnestly praying for there to be another way to accomplish this. Jesus's prayer shows us a man entirely committed to God and accomplishing God's will—no matter the cost. A friend of mine once shared that he never asks God for what he wants. Instead, he goes to God and asks for God's will. To be clear, I do think it is okay to go to God with our desires, yet it should be done with a posture of surrender to God's will and not to our own. God promises "that if we ask anything according to his will, he hears us" (1 John 5:14), and "he will give you [those who delight in him] the desires of your heart" (Psalm 37:4).

Jesus's prayer shows us a man entirely committed to accomplishing God's will.

Jesus models acceptance toward God's will, even at the detriment of the desires of his heart. Through prayer and the power of the Holy Spirit Jesus allowed himself to be arrested, spoke with authority to the high council in Jerusalem, proclaimed his true identity as Messiah to Pilate the Roman governor, listened to the angry screams of the people he came to save, offered a prayer of forgiveness for those who persecuted him, and suffered and died a painful yet purposeful death to save all of creation. You do not always get to know the purpose of a situation as Jesus did, but through prayer you can gain trust in his overall purpose for the greater mission over your life.

Response

Last, Jesus prayed to God, and God responded. The angel appeared to Jesus, and the Holy Spirit provided strength to Jesus to fulfill his purpose (Luke 22:43). William Barclay points out that Jesus enters into his time of prayer in darkness with fear but comes out in the light and with peace *because of* his conversation with God.[3] God did not change the plan, just as God did not change my situation with my mom. However, God is faithful, and just as he provided strength for Jesus and comfort for me, he will provide what you need through the Spirit to accomplish the mission and purpose he has for your life.

As Jesus said at the Last Supper, you "do not belong to the world, just as I do not belong to the world" (John 17:16 NRSVUE). You belong to God. Your purpose is to help fulfill God's mission to "go and make disciples of all nations" (Matthew 28:19). Jesus explicitly states that you will "face persecution" in this world (John 16:33 NRSVUE). Our mission is to go into this world by the power of the Holy Spirit and become more Christlike. This does not mean a life of no suffering, for Christ himself suffered. This does not mean a life of complete comfort either, for Christ himself did not live a life of comfort. This does not mean a life of happiness, for Christ himself, though he prayed often, did not live a life of complete happiness.

Just as I have experienced times of suffering, like losing my mother at such a young age, or times of joys, like becoming a mother myself, it is imperative to remember your purpose. As you exist in this world, may God go before you, beside you, and with you as you go to him in authentic prayer, sharing your desires and accepting his response, trusting that he will respond through the Spirit who will, on our behalf, intercede with God.

---

1. What does prayer look like in your faith community?
2. Do you feel free to express difficult or vulnerable emotions during prayer? How does your body feel if you pray in this way?
3. Do you know someone who models praying for their desires but with a posture of surrender? What does that look like?

Explore: Write out one of your own prayers focusing on your desires and emotions. Next, read a prayer from the Book of Common Prayer (available for free online). Reflect on how you respond to each of these types of prayers.

Chapter 28

Jesus Was Abandoned by Many

MELISSA PILLMAN

> *At noon, darkness fell across the whole land until three o'clock. Then at three o'clock Jesus called out with a loud voice, "Eloi, Eloi, lema sabachthani?" which means "My God, my God, why have you abandoned me?"*
>
> —MARK 15:33–34 (NLT)

I love pleasing people. If you know the language of personality profiling, I'm an Enneagram 2, which means I *love* to help others. But more than that, I *need to be needed by others* or I can't figure out what to do with myself. My love language is words of affirmation, so I love to *hear* that I am needed by someone and that I was helpful to them. The outcome of this combination is that it makes me very happy to make people happy.

My teenage kids have caught hold of this fact and are known to use "mom keywords" to get what they want: "Mom, will you be the bestest helper and do my laundry for me? I *need* you!" As a mom, I fall for it every time. As a pastor, I have had to get used to the idea that I will not always succeed at helping people in the ways they hoped I would. I'm willing to muscle through the conflict and disappointment that come from that, but I also try to avoid it whenever possible.

Not so with Jesus. During his ministry on earth, he was prepared to stay true to a singular task—doing the will of the Father. When we read of the miracles he performed, and the crowds who gathered to hear his teaching, we might think that Jesus enjoyed the approval of the masses. After all, his life (and death and resurrection) on earth prompted a new movement of faith that would become the largest religion in the world (according to my quick Google search)! It might therefore come as a shock to learn that Jesus wasn't winning popularity contests in the ancient Mediterranean world. He was followed by some, but he also experienced resistance, betrayal, denial, and even abandonment by those closest to him.

Turning Their Backs on Jesus

Most of us know that Jesus angered many of the Jewish religious leaders of his time with his words and actions, especially as he challenged them beyond their rule following to expose hearts that had become proud and hypocritical. The gospel of Matthew records a moment when Jesus miraculously heals a man's lame hand with his word on the Sabbath (a Jewish day of rest when work was forbidden), and the religious leaders' immediate response is to start plotting how to *kill Jesus* (12:9–14)! That seems a bit extreme to my modern eyes, but we see such reactions again and again through the gospel accounts of Jesus's earthly ministry. We can imagine that he made some pretty real enemies because we know that he was sent to the cross to die a criminal's death, even when he had committed no crime according to Roman law. Sure, we know he had *those* enemies. But didn't everyone else love Jesus? He was blessing children and healing paralytics, right? Yes, but he was also speaking a message about the kingdom of God with a system of ethics countercultural to life under foreign Roman rule. Jesus's Jewish followers were looking for a Savior and they got one, but not in the way that they imagined. So Jesus came speaking love and hope and grace, but this "rescue plan" was not looking at all as the people expected. Jesus knew he wasn't pleasing people; he was in the business of pleasing his Father.

Jesus often taught in parables, that is, stories that represent something deeper than the surface meaning. People loved to sit and listen to him teach, and he became quite renowned and gained a following. And they really loved to witness miracles! At one point in John's gospel, we see that a great crowd was following Jesus (over five thousand men plus an unknown number of women and children) and he miraculously provided food for them all until they were satisfied . . . from only five loaves of bread and two fish (6:1–15). But then he spoke metaphorically about the better life-giving sustenance that God was providing through Christ—his own body and blood given as the "bread" of life. Well, that freaked out plenty of people. Many of his own disciples deserted him (verse 66). Even his brothers thought he was "out of his mind" (Mark 3:21). His own family doubted him.

Jesus knew he wasn't pleasing people; he was in the business of pleasing his Father.

Jesus invested deeply into the lives of the men and women who followed him; they were not only his disciples but also his friends. They were the ones who were with him day in and day out, sharing meals and travel and stories with one another as they learned from their teacher. Their relationships included a bond of loyalty and commitment. But even those close companions of Jesus would abandon him at the end of his life. One disciple betrayed him, turning him in to his enemies in exchange for a bribe (Luke 22:4); one of his closest friends, Peter, denied even knowing him after pledging to follow Jesus even unto death if needed (Mark 14:29–31; John 18:17, 25–27). And in the moment of his arrest, *all* his disciples deserted him (Mark 14:50).

Jesus accepted all this as part of the cost of his mission. Jesus was not a people pleaser—he was faithful to the will of the Father. The loss, desertion, betrayal, abandonment, and denial Jesus faced at the hands of family, friends, and followers would not deter him from his ministry. I imagine it all hurt while it was happening. I think of that sometimes when my heart is aching; Jesus knows *all* my hurts and has experienced them firsthand from his own relationships. But there is one hurt that I simply cannot imagine: Jesus felt abandoned by God.

When Jesus Cried Out

What? How could Jesus ever feel abandoned by God? After all, Jesus *is* God! Yes, and from eternity past, the Father and Son (along with the Spirit) have been in perfect relational unity. There was never a time when God was *not* Father, Son, and Holy Spirit together as God. The theological term for their relationship is *perichoresis*, meaning the metaphorical dance of self-giving love that defines the relationship of the Trinity even now! But in one horrific moment, as the faithful Son cried out on the cross, "My God, my God, why have you abandoned me?" (Mark 15:34 NLT), we hear the pain of Jesus's feeling of separation from triune perichoresis.

It's easy to see this moment of perceived abandonment with shock, as if a mean Father betrayed a faithful Son. As a mom, that thought disturbs me—would I ever turn my back to my hurting children crying out to me, holding out their hands to be held, as if I was "teaching them a lesson" by showing them my *wrath*?! Of course not, but that's not what's happening here either. Remember, Father, Son, and Spirit are together God; they are all God. So when Jesus's "self" walked to the cross willingly and faithfully, that was *God's* "self" walking to the cross willingly and faithfully. That's why we say we see the love of God through Jesus's sacrifice. The only one who could bridge the chasm between a holy triune God and a broken, sinful world was God. God loved us enough to experience a sense of abandonment for the first and only time in history (past or future) so that we could forever rest assured that we are never abandoned by God. Christ's moment of abandonment created a path so that we might know we'll forever be reconciled with God (2 Corinthians 5:18–21). We can never again be separated from God:

> No, in all these things we are more than conquerors through him who loved us. For I am convinced that neither death nor life, neither angels nor demons, neither the present nor the future, nor any powers, neither height nor depth, nor anything else in all creation, will be able to separate us from the love of God that is in Christ Jesus our Lord. (Romans 8:37–39)

Wait, don't rush past that. Read Paul's words again, but slowly. Yes, Jesus cried out that he felt separated from the triune love dance, but he paid that cosmic price to show his love to you. In that cry, in that horrid moment, do you see the beauty of how Jesus addresses God? "My God, my God." Even in utter distress, the Son continues to claim God as "my" God.[1] Devotion in the face of abandonment.

We see Jesus continue to love us with that same reckless devotion every day. In my Enneagram 2 language, Jesus was, and is, the ultimate helper to those of us who are so very needy. We may deny his presence, desert his teaching, abandon our prayer habits, and reject his love, and yet still he remains devoted, forever serving in love as the forger of a path back, time and time again, to our loving God.

---

1. What aspects of Jesus's ministry pull in your interest and which aspects push away your interest? Are there difficult teachings from Jesus that you wish you could ignore? Who can you talk with about these teachings?
2. Who in your community may feel abandoned? Do you identify with feelings of abandonment? Is it possible to sense divine love in the midst of feeling abandoned?

3. Prophets frequently describe feelings of abandonment, and their God-given mission often looked like a failure to those around them. What does this reveal about our communities and social ideals? Who do you know that speaks prophetically and may encounter feelings of abandonment?

Explore: Read or listen to a story about a Christian who suffered significant rejection, such as early Christian martyrs Perpetua or Blandina, or more recently Watchman Nee or Sabrina Wurmbrand. Reflect on God's presence in their lives, regardless of outward circumstances. Consider how a community of Christians might have entered into their experience to support them.

Chapter 29

Jesus Was Veil Tearing

HEATHER HART

> *O God of unchangeable power and eternal light . . . let the whole world see and know that things which were cast down are being raised up, and things which had grown old are being made new, and that all things are being brought to their perfection by him through whom all things were made, your Son Jesus Christ our Lord.*
>
> —The Book of Common Prayer

My son's arm bent at a terrible angle. His blue eyes widened in terror, and his shriek reverberated through the emergency room. I gripped the edge of the hospital bed, inches from his face, locked onto his eyes. I would not be leaving. He trusted me, yet this pain was unlike anything he'd known before. His arm was broken, and we needed an X-ray. He was five years old and all he could do was scream in agony. We would soon be escorted into emergency surgery that resulted in pins and a cast. His first day of kindergarten would come in a couple of weeks, but before any of that could happen, we needed this X-ray of his arm. We needed a vision of the damage and the path for healing.

The tearing of the temple veil at Jesus's crucifixion gives a vision of both damage and healing. This event, filled with symbolism and significance, uncovers the depth of corruption permeating creation and the method of restoration. A similar tearing also happened earlier in Jesus's story at his baptism. The Greek verb *schizo*, "to tear, split,"[1] only appears in two scenes in the gospel of Mark: the opening of the heavens at Jesus's baptism (1:10) and with the tearing of the temple veil at his death (15:38). In several ways, the heavens "tearing" at Jesus's baptism serves as a guide for understanding the tearing in the temple.[2]

Baptismal Tearing

The gospel of Mark loves symbolism and highlighting similar types of people and events. In Mark 1:4 we meet John the Baptist as he "appeared in the wilderness preaching a baptism of repentance for the forgiveness of sins." John's location hints at Israel's wandering in the wilderness, and his attire—camel's hair and a leather belt (verse 6)—alludes to the clothes of a prophet who speaks from God (e.g., Elijah in 2 Kings 1:6). The description of John in Mark is full of imagery and significance, and his action of baptizing carries this weight as well.

Immersion in water carried symbolic meaning for ancient Jews. In the first century, Jewish people were not frequently baptized as an indication of spiritual repentance. However, Jewish people did regularly immerse themselves in water as a part of their religious expression.[3] Those listening to John were familiar with Jewish purification washings that declared them "clean" and meant they were prepared to appear before the holy presence of God.[4] While uncleanness could arise from wrongdoing, in many cases uncleanness arose from normal life experiences without any implication of sin. Those who prepared a dead body for burial, women who had given birth, and those with skin diseases experienced uncleanness and needed ritual immersion for purity.[5] These frequent ritual cleansings were often done in a special bath called a *mikvah*. This same word is used to describe the gathering of water in Genesis 1:9–10, when dry land appears and is declared good.[6] The Jewish people hearing John the Baptist's proclamation would have known that immersion was periodically required to restore religious purity and that this purity was God's "good" creation.

Additionally, John's listeners knew first-century Gentiles who converted to Judaism from paganism were baptized to become part of the Jewish community.[7] This was a normal event at conversion. They also knew that John's location at the Jordan River was not accidental. It invoked the Israelite crossing of the Jordan before entering the promised land, a special moment leading to a new age of God's people. John's baptism is a physical act alluding to spiritual cleanness, conversion, and the new era to come. In this swirl of ideas, John proclaims a unique onetime immersion, a baptism for repentance and the forgiveness of sins. This is a special act. It stood as a decisive turning point in a person's life. According to John, the day of the Lord approached, and the faithful remnant of Israel must be morally cleansed to be ready.[8] John's actions moved beyond purification rituals and declared something definitive was needed for God's people. God was coming near in a powerful new way, and it was imperative to be ready.

Like other Jewish people listening to John, Jesus came to the Jordan River and was baptized as a member of God's holy people in preparation for this new age of God's presence.[9] Jesus exemplified faithful Israel, yet unlike those around him Jesus was not waiting for the new era John preached about. Jesus *was* the new era. The day of the Lord arrived in the person of Jesus. Just as Joshua had led the Israelites out of the wilderness, across the Jordan River, and into the promised land, so the gospel of Mark connects Jesus with leading the faithful out of their present age and into a new experience of God. For true flourishing, humanity needed something beyond the maintenance of regular purity rituals. It needed God's creative presence. It needed re-creation. It needed to cross the Jordan River into the promised land.

According to Mark, when Jesus emerged from the water, the heavens were torn open in an apocalyptic moment: an unveiling of heavenly realities (1:10–11). This is an inside look at things normally unseen—a vision of God at work.[10] This work rips open the divide between heaven and earth. At this moment, the Spirit descends and God declares love for and approval of the Son. Mark's scene is rife with imagery from Isaiah 64:1, which appeals for the heavens to burst open and for God to come down and bring salvation. This salvation is a new activity of the Spirit, similar in type to the Spirit hovering before creation in Genesis 1:2 but now resting on Jesus and anointing him for his task.[11] When Jesus emerges from the Jordan, it is not the river that parts but rather the heavens. God's movement has come into the earthly realm, set wild in the world.[12] Salvation will be a re-creation begun through Jesus.

The prophesied new age of God's presence begins with Jesus, and the heavenly veil tears to show the dramatic dawning of a new defining moment at his baptism. The beloved Son marks the beginning of re-creation. What has been torn is not easily closed back up; what God is doing is not something that will be undone. Mark's good news is that the anointed one, the Son of God who brings the promised salvation and judgment of evil, has arrived.[13]

What has been torn is not easily closed back up; what God is doing is not something that will be undone.

Jesus's baptism tears open the heavens and, in turn, Jesus's death tears open the veil in the temple. Like Mark's story of Jesus's baptism, the gospel's account of the temple and the veil is layered with symbolic significance. In Genesis 1:26–28 humanity is created in the image of God and given the directive to be fruitful and increase in number, to fill the earth and subdue it. As God's representatives, humanity serves on God's behalf by expanding the good order of creation throughout the earth.[14] In Genesis 2:15 before Eve is created, the man is directed to work (*'abad*) and care (*shamar*) for the garden.

Those two Hebrew verbs for "work" and "care" used in this verse, often translated "till" and "keep" in the agricultural context of Genesis 2:15, are also frequently used in the Old Testament in reference to serving and guarding God's Word and the priestly activities involved in maintaining the temple.[15] In that manner, Adam and Eve's responsibilities were layered with spiritual meaning. These Genesis scenes point to humanity working alongside God's good order to maintain purity and to expand it. The stories of cosmic creation and the garden of Eden are reflected in the structure and decor of the temple. The temple structure is the place where God and humanity meet, much like the cosmic scene in Genesis 1 and the garden where Adam and Eve meet with God.[16]

Breaking Through

In the temple structure, the holy of holies represented the invisible heavenly realm where God lives.[17] The high priest only entered this section once a year. Outside of the holy of holies was the holy place, an area with furniture symbolic of earthly functions and only served by priests. The holy place contained representations of light and food associated with human habitation. Long ago, in the original temple, the holy of holies held the ark of the covenant associated with the divine presence.[18] Separating the holy of holies from the holy place was a carefully woven linen veil about forty-two feet long and six feet wide. This temple veil figuratively separated the heavens and the earth by visually separating the two areas and shielding the holy of holies from view. This curtain of separation required skilled craftsmen to weave in blue, purple, and scarlet yarns and embroidered images of angelic guards (Exodus 26:31), possibly a reference to the starry heavens and the cherubim guarding Eden.[19]

According to the Synoptic Gospels, when Jesus died on the cross, the temple veil tore from top to bottom (Matthew 27:51; Mark 15:38; Luke 23:45). The heavy curtain ripped, invoking imagery of the cosmos rending in two, revealing what was once concealed, and releasing what was once constrained.[20] These gospel accounts give us a physical event with deep theological implications, both positive and negative. Both Jesus's baptism and his death emphasize insight into the typically unseen heavenly realm—a new revelation.

Jesus's choice to suffer and die on the cross reveals the depth of God's love that reaches out across a sin-infected world to bring restoration. God himself tears the veil of separation, unwilling to let creation continue in decay. God's love is on full display. As Hebrews 12:2 beautifully reminds us, Jesus—the author and perfecter of faith—endured the cross, scorned its shame, and sat down at the right hand of the throne of God because of the joy to come. Jesus undid the corruption permeating humanity to bring about a renewed people connected to God, a renewed creation no longer mired in destruction. This renewal, the overhaul and reconstitution of the world, brings God joy and was worth the painful tearing.

Jesus undid the corruption permeating humanity to bring about a renewed people connected to God, a renewed creation no longer mired in destruction.

Further, the tearing of the temple veil is a visual symbol that God's presence is no longer confined to the holy of holies but has broken out into the world bringing goodness and order out of chaos. The beginnings of re-creation alluded to at Jesus's baptism continue with the divine presence filling the world in a new way. God has burst through the barrier, rushing the world with his divine presence. Tearing the veil points to direct access to God in the new re-creation. Jesus, the faithful new Adam, begins a new humanity who can connect with God as directly and intimately as in the original garden. There is a new and personal closeness with God.

In light of this irreversible renewal, the original temple system is judged and rendered obsolete; the old structure has passed away. God has left the old temple, and the new temple begins in Jesus. The reality of the new temple encompasses Jesus reaching out and restoring, bringing order and goodness, filling the earth, connecting with humanity, expanding access to God, and bringing judgment.

Conversely, a torn veil differs significantly from a veil that is simply pushed open. This veil is destroyed from top to bottom. It wasn't merely a cloudy day when Jesus died; darkness covered the land. This was a day when everything turned inside out. Day turned into night, the rocks split, and the earth quaked. Tombs were opened and the dead were raised. This is imagery of the very order of the cosmos tearing at the seams. The rebirth of creation is judgment on the severity of the corruption saturating it. The torn veil is necessary because the decay of corruption is so pervasive that it cannot be escaped or tamped down. The problem of corruption is not merely a minor dislocation fixed with a gentle tug. For humanity to be near to God and join in God's expansive goodness, the prison of decay must be utterly destroyed through the act of renewal. This is the vision of the damage: the very cosmos is ripped in half to undo the injury. The only healing path forward is re-creation.

Tearing Renews Our Vision

My son had been with our beloved babysitter when he slipped off the monkey bars and fell that night. I saw her missed calls and rushed straight home. When I initially saw his tear-streaked face and arm propped up with pillows, I feebly hoped it was just a dislocation that could be fixed quickly. I didn't want him to be in pain, and I wanted it to be remedied easily. Both of these proved untrue. His pain was overwhelming, and an ambulance ride followed by emergency surgery were necessary. I'm thankful for the wisdom of doctors who saw the X-ray and knew surgery could not wait. Eventually, the cast came off and the pins came out. His arm healed well because they had the vision to see what was broken and took action.

Spiritual vision doesn't come naturally in a world still seeping with decay. The definitive death blow to corruption has been dealt by Jesus, yet God's renewal hasn't infiltrated every corner of creation. Evil still exists. Terrible things still happen. We, the followers of Jesus, need renewed vision that lets us see the damage and the healing. The presence of God that tore through the temple veil is alive and working. It is this presence that brings us both renewal and vision.

We must continue to remind each other that we are filled with the Spirit, being renewed and enabled to see with spiritual eyes. With these eyes we can see the decay shaping the world around us, manipulating people, systems, and circumstances, sowing deceit and strife. We must ask the Spirit to reveal true insight to us, to show us what is not apparent, so we can understand the full extent of the damage. Through Bible study, our faith communities, and our personal connection with the Spirit, we can gain insight. Enabled by the Spirit, we may speak humbly and yet courageously point out the corruption and decay in our midst.

We need to understand the damage because we cling to the truth that God declared humanity and the world worth saving. We must seek to share God's love for all people by participating in God's work. We need to ask to be filled with love for all of God's good creation. As Jesus's followers, we are free to join in wherever we see God working in our local area.

We must also ask the Spirit to help each of us to experience personal closeness with God and the community of faith. We need to remind ourselves that the old order of separation has passed away and God has come near. Even when we cannot feel God or see God at work, we can know that God *is* close and *is* working. We are lovingly connected to God, and God cares about each one of us. We matter and are known as unique individuals.

Finally, we remember that what we see in this earthly world is not a complete picture of reality. We must place our trust, our ultimate allegiance, in God, not in any current media personality, human-made institution, or national program. We need to always turn our face toward Jesus and yearn for him over and above any person or idea that seeks to capture our hope. Only Jesus is our hope, our path for healing. And we must pray as he taught us: "Your [God's] kingdom come, your will be done, on earth as it is in heaven" (Matthew 6:10).

---

1. Have you had an experience where a deeper spiritual reality suddenly became apparent? How did your body and emotions respond in that moment? Who or what helps you understand that moment correctly?
2. Who in your community is helpful at understanding biblical symbolism? What personal habits or tools help you make sense of ancient imagery?
3. Does your faith community explore the implications of "re-creation"? What does it look like in your neighborhood to join in God's rebirth of creation?

Explore: Write a list of creative activities that feel like a way to participate in God's re-creation of the world. Invite a friend to try one of these with you.

Chapter 30

Jesus Was Instrumental in Our Adoption

ADRIENNE GIBSON

We wait eagerly for our adoption to sonship, the redemption of our bodies.

—Romans 8:23

Adoption can be both a beautiful undertaking and a complicated mess, and unsurprisingly there is a significant bundle of emotions wrapped up in this word. The word *adoption* can make someone feel welcome. It can also make someone feel alone or unloved. Children who share their adoption stories with me often struggle to do so, as do most adults.

I once worked with a sixteen-year-old girl who had been adopted at birth. When she was very young her birth parents had another little girl, and this sister was adopted by a different family. Social services put these two adoptive families together, and a few times each year the girls would get together. For an adoptee this was an amazing situation, as she had a full-blood sister in her life. Yet she despised seeing her sister, and she often spoke about feeling forced to have this person in her life. This feeling probably came from what this sister reminded her of every time they got together—that she was adopted.

As someone with eighteen-plus years in the social services field, I also come to the word *adoption* with a complicated and mixed set of emotions. In the modern era, the understanding of adoption is that it is a solution for an unfathomable problem. When a child is adopted, it has to be acknowledged that there was first a rejection before there was a choosing or accepting. What many of us fail to recognize is that adoption is the best solution to a horrible problem.[1] Adopted children are chosen by their adoptive parents, which is beautiful and redeeming. Maybe the word *chosen* is a complicated or heavy word to use in this situation, but what I mean is that adoptive parents have agency and voice in this situation. Adoptive children do not. It is this "choosing" that has taken place to be accepted into a new family that has happened. The adoptive parents chose to open their home and heart to a child who needed one. But the choosing came second. What cannot be overlooked is that before they were chosen, they were forsaken. This is the truth that is hard. This is the reality that wounds. This is where those adopted need deep healing. Adoption creates wounds.

Should all of us who are faithful followers of Jesus Christ as our redeemer feel wounded? Were we rejected before we were chosen? Truly, I think I have misunderstood what it means to be adopted by God through Christ when I look at this word through modern eyes.

Adoption in the Greco-Roman World

Let's take a step back in time to look at adoption during the birth of Christianity in the ancient Mediterranean world. It is imperative to understand these differences so we have a clearer understanding of the word *adoption*. Infant mortality in the Greco-Roman world was high. It is estimated that as many as 50 percent of children during this time period did not live past the age of five.[2] With the infant mortality rate being so high, a father had to worry about the *oikos*, the family or household, and its survival and support in old age.[3] The continuation of a man's family line was of supreme importance. The

Greco-Roman world also maintained an honor-versus-shame culture, such that children were begotten in the hopes that they would bring a family honor, but there was also the risk that a child might bring a family shame. When the high infant mortality rate and the potential for shame are put together, it is a recipe for disaster.

A father's power was most visibly seen within the family structure during the birth of a child, as the father held the power to accept that child into the family or to reject that child.[4] A rejected child would often be put outside the home, essentially a form of child abandonment called "exposure," and either perished or was taken in as a slave by another household. Now, considering how important the family line was within Greco-Roman culture, what did an ancient family do if their children did not live past the age of five, or if their birth children were rejected by the father? This is where adoption comes into the picture. Adoption was the common solution for handpicking an heir. It gave men the power to choose an individual who was honorable and worthy to take on the family name and line. Often fathers would adopt grown men who had proven themselves worthy. One of the most well-known examples of this is when Caesar Augustus was adopted by his great-uncle Julius Caesar. Especially among elite families, adoption was also used to secure a smooth and valuable succession of power and wealth.[5]

Adoption in the Old Testament

When I think of having another father apart from my biological father, I first think of the Lord's Prayer. Jesus tells his disciples in Matthew 6 to start their prayer with the words, "Our Father." The Lord's Prayer is not found in the Old Testament, but let's briefly investigate how the ancient Israelites addressed the concept of God as Father. Would the ancient Israelites have understood this idea of God being their Father? In Exodus 4:22–23 Moses relays God's message to Pharaoh, which refers to Israel as "my firstborn son." This concept is seen again in Hosea 11:1, where God says to the prophet: "When Israel was a child, I loved him and out of Egypt I called my son." The Israelites saw God as Creator, King, *and* Father, and they saw themselves as adoptive children of God because he rescued them out of Egypt.[6]

God the Father was also the Father to the king of Israel. Psalm 89 speaks of the covenant God made with the "chosen one" (verse 3), the king of Israel, and the line of David. Yahweh is the Father to the Israelites and to the Davidic king. The Old Testament sets the stage for the understanding of Jesus as the son of David and as the embodiment for Israel as a whole.[7] They shared the same Father.

Adoption in the New Testament

In the Gospels, Jesus uses paternal language several times to portray the relationships he shared with God, his disciples, and his followers. In Luke 2:49 a twelve-year-old Jesus speaks to his parents after they find him in the temple. He tells them they should have known he would be in his Father's house. After Jesus is baptized, a voice is heard calling Jesus "My Son" (Matthew 3:17). In Matthew 12:50 Jesus speaks of God as his Father, stating that whoever does the will of God the Father should see themselves as Jesus's brother, sister, and mother. This is family language being used to portray God, Jesus, and his followers. Jesus wanted to make very clear that he is in the family line of God because he was fully God. Yet he also wanted his disciples and followers, including you and me, to know that *we* are also wanted in the family line of God. I believe John's gospel is the first to make this declaration: "Yet to all who did receive him, to those who believed in his name, he gave the right to become children of God—children born not of natural descent, nor of human decision or a husband's will, but born of God" (1:12–13). God is declaring that we are his. He desires us; he is calling us to join his family.

Paul was a faithful Jew who was taught from an early age the concept of Yahweh as his Father and of the people of Israel as the adopted children of their rescuer and redeemer. Paul's writings help us understand more clearly the concept of biblical adoption. His writings shed light on who is adopted, who is doing the adopting, and how this act is possible. Romans 8:14–17 states that everyone led by the Spirit of God is now a child of God. Everyone is being offered the gift of the Spirit, and by receiving the Spirit we are adopted by God. The Spirit is made possible to us by the life, death, and resurrection of Jesus, who with his sacrifice brought about humanity's ability to be adopted children. As a result, we are now children of God. This takes us back to what being adopted in the Greco-Roman world meant—adoption makes a child an heir of the father. We are members of God's family. Since we are heirs, we now have all rights and responsibilities of that family. We are not adopted by Jesus; we are adopted by God. Yet that adoption is only made possible by Jesus's death and resurrection. We are now co-heirs with Jesus.

We are now children of God.

Paul speaks again about our adoption in Galatians 3:28: "There is neither Jew nor Gentile, neither slave nor free, nor is there male and female, for you are all one in Christ Jesus. If you belong to Christ, then you are Abraham's seed, and heirs according to the promise." God promised Abraham a family, and it is through Christ that this large family is finally coming to fruition. Everyone is now on even ground, and we are all part of Abraham's family. Jesus as Messiah made all that possible. Paul also wants to point out that sonship has deep meaning. We are heirs and we have an intimacy with our Father.

Paul continues explaining sonship in Galatians 4:6–7: "Because you are his sons, God sent the Spirit of his Son into our hearts, the Spirit who calls out, '*Abba*, Father.' So you are no longer a slave, but God's child; and since you are his child, God has made you also an heir." We were enslaved to something before our adoption, and that is what we are being taken back from. These verses speak the language of exodus, of being a rescued people and of being brought out of slavery and given the law and an inheritance—the promised land.[8] The journey for all believers is like this exodus story. Many of us have become slaves to self, because what we often worship is ourselves and our own abilities. We are slaves to our thinking that we can fulfill our own needs and that we know right from wrong apart from God. Like the Israelites were rescued from slavery in Egypt and adopted by Yahweh, who loved them and cared for them, we are also being rescued from our own slavery and adopted into this family line.

Our Adoption

We are all invited into the family of God. What this entails for you and for me are all the rights and privileges that come along with being a full heir of a family. There may be hurt or pain for some of us. There is new life and rejoicing in this adoption, but there is pain and loss for the humanity around us that does not accept this adoption. And we too, like the sixteen-year-old girl mentioned earlier, are often going to be faced with the painful reminder that some have chosen the adoption and others have not. But this is a different kind of pain and loss.

Adoption is a gift, one offered to every human. This adoption through Christ differs from the modern understanding of adoption, because this adoption is our choice. We have agency and voice in our adoption process. This is the human story of how we get rescued. Jesus's life, death, resurrection, and ascension are what make this story come to its culmination. Adoption is made possible through Jesus of Nazareth.

---

1. What is your experience with contemporary adoption? How do contemporary adoption practices affect your community?
2. What linguistic characteristics feel most important for understanding what Jesus meant when he refers to God as "Father" in

the Gospels? Which aspects of Roman adoption feel most important for understanding adoption in Paul's letters?

3. Consider how different people in your community might respond to the language of "adoption" in a church service. How might your faith-based community care for different people while exploring this metaphor?

Explore: Read a memoir or listen to a podcast describing the life of someone who experienced contemporary adoption, such as *Born Broken: An Adoptive Journey* by Kristen Berry or the podcast *Adoption: The Long View* with Lori Holden. Pay attention to your body and emotions. Consider how this experience affects a person's perception of God.

Chapter 31

Jesus Was the Word

TYLER CALLAHAN

In the beginning was the Word, and the Word was with God, and the Word was God.
—JOHN 1:1

"The Word of God is inspired, inerrant, and infallible. And when he was about eighteen years old, he grew a beard."[1] This cutting one-liner from Brad Jersak is bound to draw some head scratches and double takes. But it's more than a clever quip; it's a necessary challenge to an assumption many of us adopted early on in our Christian walks—when we refer to "the Word of God," we are first and foremost referring to *the Bible.*

"What's the big deal?" you might ask. Well, it's more than a simple matter of vocabulary. Our gradual shift away from Jesus, whom the Bible refers to as "the Word" (John 1:1), toward Scripture as "the Word" is evidence of a larger issue in our individual and corporate spirituality. Simply put, *we've made an idol out of the Bible.* Some scholars refer to this as "biblicism."

Placing the Bible over Jesus

American sociologist Christian Smith describes biblicism as "a theory about the Bible that emphasizes together its exclusive authority, infallibility, perspicuity, self-sufficiency, internal consistency, self-evident meaning, and universal applicability."[2]

On the surface, these assumptions might not sound so bad—you might've even heard a few of these ideas taught from the pulpit once or twice. But when we look closely, we see a thought process that, if not kept in check, can grow to silence the witness of Jesus and the voice of the Spirit in our lives today. Put another way, these assumptions can quickly turn into stepping stones toward a hermeneutic that takes the Word of God (Jesus) and shackles him to the pages of the Bible, effectively placing God under *our* control and keeping his authority over our lives confined to the boundaries of our personal thoughts, feelings, and interpretations of Scripture.

Two issues commonly crop up in our faith communities when biblicism is the law of the land. First, biblicism enables Christians to pick and choose whichever "clear commands" from Scripture fit their preexisting opinions, claiming them to be "universally applicable," while writing off the passages that challenge their perspectives as "unique to their time." Take the role of women in ministry, for instance. Some have been quick to quote the "plain" statements from Paul when discussing if or how women should be allowed to lead, but they ignore the Bible's own witness to women like Phoebe and Priscilla, who were *commended* by Paul for their leadership in the early church (Romans 16:1, 3).

The second issue is that despite all its claims about "democratic perspicuity" and "commonsense hermeneutics" (e.g., anyone can pick this up and understand it without needing any further education), biblicism still hasn't been able to present "one coherent, much less comprehensive social ethic to guide a compelling 'biblical' response to contemporary social problems."[3] This point is at the heart of what's turning out to be a generational crisis of faith for many young people. American Christians today simply cannot agree about how the church should respond to pressing social issues like immigration, sexuality, policing, and the ever-widening gap between the rich and poor. Various groups claim to have the "biblical" solution, but they seem to miss the ironic fact that other Christian groups are using the same Bible to come up with their opposing view. And here's the worst part: while we lock ourselves away in our sanctuaries to argue about "what the Bible clearly says," nonreligious groups are actually *doing* something about the injustices they see in the world.

To be fair, biblicism is most often the result of well-intentioned engagement with Scripture that has simply overcorrected against the interpretive challenges on the other side of the spectrum. A desire for deeper reverence turns into an unintentional hierarchy of the sacraments. A desire to encourage daily reading leads us to oversimplify *what* we're reading, assuming it should make sense to us today without much effort or additional study. The desire to uphold the Bible as trustworthy leads us to ignore or diminish (or, in other words, to tame) the chaotic, confusing, and seemingly contradictory statements of Scripture. The true Word of God, however, is wild and untamable, and he's never as we expect him to be.

We want a lion, but we get a lamb (John 1:29).

We want a warrior, but he tells us to turn the other cheek (Matthew 5:39).

We want a political revolutionary, but he dies at the hands of the empire (Matthew 27:32–56).

Upholding Jesus as the Word

Believing that Jesus is the true Word of God requires us to acknowledge that whatever we believe about God (and, by extension, ourselves) must be rooted in the picture of Jesus we see in the Scriptures. But at the same time, we must be open to the possibility that God may want to do "a new thing" (Isaiah 43:19) in our time and place. Furthermore, we must pay constant attention to our temptation to substitute the *Word* for the *words of Jesus* out of a subconscious desire to shape God into our own image.

For instance, the Old Testament depictions of a wrathful and furious God have been difficult for many Christians today to reconcile with the picture of Jesus we see in the New Testament. Within the Western, post-Enlightenment stream of Christianity, we've responded to this dilemma in a number of ways—some good, some not so good. On our brighter days, we've come to accept that God is infinitely complex, and that in order for God to be good, he must be just. We've then sought to see how the violent depictions of God in the Old Testament are reflections of his justice but have been forced to accept a level of "mystery" when it comes to depictions of God-ordained genocide, including the murder of women and children (1 Samuel 15:3). On our darker days, we've looked to those same, violent pictures of God and used them as permission slips to carry out heinous acts of violence ourselves.

Whatever we believe about God must be rooted in the picture of Jesus we see in the Scriptures.

If Jesus really was the true Word of God, and the Word was with God from the beginning, and the Word *was* God (John 1:1), then perhaps any picture we have of God that doesn't look like Jesus (and more specifically, Jesus on the cross) is actually distorted. Perhaps one who inflicts violence on others, a literal fire-rainer, brings the fire upon himself. Perhaps God is calling us into a radical love that would die for our enemies, no matter how badly it burns. Perhaps when things aren't adding up, God is beckoning us to *look deeper* and invite him to speak into these gut-wrenching "mysteries" and reveal more of himself to us.

If we decide to let go of our flat readings of Scripture and give Jesus back his title as the true Word of God, we may begin to find that the Spirit is speaking a fresh word to us, here and now. After all, if the way of Jesus is the way of life and truth (John 14:6), shouldn't that way have something to say about the problems we're facing today? Generationally, we seem to talk past each other on this point. Generally speaking, younger folks are consumed with older folks' lacking response to contemporary injustices, while older folks are consumed with younger folks' lacking reverence for God. Both use the Bible (and their contextualized interpretations of it) to condemn the other. Rarely do we find the common ground that God's unifying Spirit invites us into (1 Corinthians 12:12–13). Much of this has to do with the fact that we've let the Holy Scriptures take the place of the Holy Spirit on the triune throne of authority. But if the way of Jesus has any value in the twenty-first century, it will not be in sound doctrine alone, whether theological or ethical. For Christians to have an impact on our postmodern, post-Christendom world, we need to pay attention and listen closely for what the Spirit wishes to say in our midst *right now*. And if that word aligns with the full and complete revelation of God that we see in Jesus *through* the Scriptures and is affirmed by a Spirit-led and Spirit-filled *community*, then who are we to stand in the way?

---

1. In your faith community, when someone says "the Word" does it refer to Jesus or the Bible? Have you experienced confusion with the way "the Word" as a phrase is used in your church?
2. How do your body and emotions respond when you read the list of assumptions that provide the foundation for biblicism? Are there any concepts on this list that you feel are necessary for Scripture?
3. How do your body and emotions respond to the quote, "The true Word of God, however, is wild and untamable, and he's never as we expect him to be"? Who in your faith community best displays a life that sees Jesus in this way?

Explore: Read a book or listen to a podcast that examines different assumptions about Scripture such as *How (Not) to Read the Bible* by Dan Kimball and the *BibleProject* podcast. Write out your own assumptions.

Jesus Is

Why the Life of Jesus Matters

SCOTT JOHANNINGSMEIER

> *Follow God's example, therefore, as dearly loved children and walk in the way of love, just as Christ loved us and gave himself up for us as a fragrant offering and sacrifice to God.*
>
> —EPHESIANS 5:1–2

When Susy began this journey with posting her "Jesus was" statements, one particular response appeared on almost every post that month: "Jesus *is*!" This response agreed with what was being said, whether it was "Jesus was nonviolent" or "Jesus was humble," but it demonstrated how much we focus on how we see Jesus today. However, for us to know who Jesus is today, we must turn to who Jesus was when he walked the earth.

We often take the life of Jesus for granted. Perhaps this is because we learned the stories of Jesus as children yet never allowed these stories to grow with us. Or it could be our familiarity with the life of Jesus causes us to turn to other books or passages in Scripture that "explain Jesus" rather than letting the stories in the Gospels reveal Jesus to us. Sure, year after year during Christmas and Easter we focus on who Jesus is as we celebrate his miraculous birth, sin-forgiving death, and resurrection. But the rest of the liturgical year, we often only squeeze the ministry of Jesus in whenever there is a gap between sermon series.

However, the Bible tells a different story. A great deal of the New Testament is focused on the life of Jesus. Michael Bird hits this truth head-on when he says, "The fact that you have to read four biographies of Jesus before we get to the Epistles means God might be trying to tell us something—the life of Jesus matters!"[1] Even the New Testament letters continue to look back to Jesus as the example to follow. It matters who Jesus was.

For us to know who Jesus is today, we must turn to who Jesus was.

What makes studying the life of Jesus difficult is the complexity of Jesus. Even with all the topics covered in this book, we have barely scratched the surface concerning who he was and is. We did not get into the practical aspects of Jesus, such as "Jesus was Mary's son" or "Jesus was a brother." Both of these themes are important and had an impact on Jesus's followers as the early church grew. Mary was present in the New Testament church (Acts 1:14) and would have been a source for information about Jesus.[2] Jesus's brother James became a leader of the church in Jerusalem. We also did not directly cover some of the deep theological issues surrounding Jesus, such as "Jesus was the Messiah" or "Jesus was Lord." Our list of questions about who Jesus was could go on and on.

It is impossible to get an exact model of Jesus, though many have tried. Jesus is probably the most studied and discussed person in history. The New Testament reveals much about Jesus's life, ministry, death, and resurrection, yet there is so much we do not know about him. When we read the New Testament, we find ourselves left with more questions. Many scholars and theologians have tried to "create" an accurate portrayal of the historical Jesus. Yet the results of such efforts have often resulted in portraits of Jesus that reflect the sociocultural contexts and ideologies of their authors.[3] When we consider the different ways people have understood Jesus throughout history, be it in the third-century Roman Empire, sixteenth-century Europe, or present-day America, it's not surprising that we continue to struggle with fully grasping who Jesus was and is.

Each of our contributing authors is passionate about the topics covered in this book, and it would be easy to fall into this all-too-common trap of (re-)creating Jesus the way we want to see him. Yet Susy and I challenged each of our contributors as they wrote to ground their ideas in the biblical text. To seek who Jesus was means we attempt the impossible task of removing ourselves from the equation. Yet we are all people who approach Jesus with our own personal history and worldview, and our own voices can still be found despite our best efforts. This is why reading and listening to multiple and different voices is important. Doing so provides us with thought-provoking insights and the opportunities to dialogue with one another and with the biblical text. Approaching our gospel readings honestly and with open hearts provides each of us the opportunity to grow in our own understanding of who Jesus was.

My hope is that as you read through each chapter you were challenged to grow in your understanding of Jesus (I know I was). But it is not simply enough to know who Jesus was. I think this might be the reason so many people responded with "Jesus is." Studying Jesus is not just about history—it is also about following his example and being led into a new way of thinking and living. Attempting to figure out who Jesus was is a futile exercise if it does not transform us closer and deeper into Christlikeness (Romans 12:1–2).

The New Testament letters call us to follow the example of Jesus (Ephesians 5:1–2) and to have the same mindset as Christ (Philippians 2:5). If we want to know how to follow Jesus today, we need to understand what he said and did when he was on the earth. In fact, Jesus often said, "Follow me." This was his call to the disciples (e.g., Matthew 4:19; 9:9). He would say this when people would come asking how to inherit eternal life (Mark 10:17–21). He also stressed the importance of what it meant to follow him (Mark 8:34; Luke 14:27). The call to follow Jesus today still requires knowing what he said and did in the past. Through following Jesus's example, we reorient our lives in Christlikeness.

I speak on behalf of all the contributing authors when I say our biggest prayer is that you do not stop with only reading this book. We poured into *Jesus Was* because each of us absolutely loves Jesus and we want to share the Jesus we know with you. Wherever you are in your life—a dedicated Christian, someone who has walked away from faith, or someone who has never been involved in a life of faith—we challenge you to continue pursuing Jesus, asking questions about him, and seeking who he was.

---

1. Reflect on how *Jesus Was* affected your body and emotions. Have you felt the Holy Spirit prompt you with a certain idea? Do you see your local community any differently? What aspects of Jesus's life made an impression on you?

Acknowledgments

First, a mighty thank-you to Scot McKnight for encouraging us all to write and to publish. Of course, much of the thinking and scholarship in *Jesus Was* comes from your teaching and influence. You are truly a godfather to this project, and a role model for living the way of *Jesus Was*. The Gertie Girls and Guys thank you! We also thank our other professors at Northern Seminary, with a special nod to Nijay Gupta, who encouraged us to publish this book. We also want to thank literary agent Rachelle Gardner for taking on this unique project, and our wonderful editors and the team at Kregel Publications for catching the vision too.

This book would not exist without our contributors. We love you, and we love your work here. Thank you for partnering with us in the work. We can't wait to celebrate with you!

Scott Johanningsmeier

I would like to thank Susy for challenging us to examine the Jesus of the Bible rather than relying on our assumptions. I genuinely appreciate her walking with me on this book journey from crazy idea to completion. I also want to thank my teachers throughout the years who have encouraged, supported, and challenged me to be a better writer, including Scot McKnight, Nijay Gupta, Ann Niren, and many others. I want to thank the pastors and ministers who invested in me and helped to shape me into the pastor I am today, including Darrell

James, Michael Kincer, David Wood, John Brandon, Bill Shoulta, Tim Spring, Danny Russell, and Donna Reddick. Special thanks to the American Baptist Churches of Indiana and Kentucky. I would also like to thank our church family at Culbertson Baptist Church for your continued prayer.

I do not have adequate words to describe my gratitude for the church I pastor, Elizabeth Baptist Church. The way they care and support not only me but others around them is truly remarkable. I repeatedly tell others that all pastors need to pastor a small church like Elizabeth Baptist. They are a church that lives as Jesus was.

It goes without saying, but I couldn't thank my parents enough for all they have done for me and the ways they brought me close to Jesus.

Of course, none of this would be possible without the support of my family: Jennifer, Rachel, and Rebecca. You have all stood with me throughout my ministry, seminary education, and work on *Jesus Was*. It's not always easy being a family with two bi-vocational individuals, but here we are following our calling, and I am so thankful for your love. One of my biggest prayers is that when you see me you will see someone who loves and follows after Jesus.

Susy Flory

First, a huge thank-you to Scott Johanningsmeier, who took up the calling of *Jesus Was* from my social media posts and began to preach on them. So proud and so blessed to work together with you on this book. I've learned so much from you!

As my writing takes a turn toward the theological (thanks to seven years of seminary studies), I want to thank my family and my friends for encouraging me to follow this dream. As long as I can remember, I've loved the Bible and loved the church. I never pass a church without noticing it and thinking about those who dreamed of it, built it, and worshipped inside of it—living out their hopes, dreams, joys, and sorrows within the kingdom represented by those walls. Every church has a story. Every church is a representation of the larger church made up of people who follow Jesus.

My father loved the church too, and while he had a regular job, his heart was always in the church. He died young at forty-seven and never got to live his dream of retiring early and going to seminary to become a pastor. He never mentioned this dream to me, but years after his death, my mom told me about it. In the flurry and worries of her last years of ill health, the story faded away for me. A few years later, I was in my local church on a Sunday morning when, right in the pew, a feeling like a very heavy blanket came over me. *I have to go to seminary.* I grabbed my phone and texted several friends, telling them what happened. "Make sure I do this," I wrote.

After my first year of seminary, which was as challenging, terrifying, and delightful as I had imagined, I decided to visit my pastor to let him know what I was doing. We had a nice talk, and he seemed happy for me. He even knew who Scot McKnight was! Then, on the way home, it happened. The conversation with my mom popped back into my mind. I relived it as I drove, her voice echoing in my ears, and then the long-forgotten memory of my dad preaching a sermon on 1 Corinthians 13, Paul's love chapter, played in my head like a movie. I burst out crying, wiping my eyes as I drove, and I kept saying to myself, *I am getting to live my dad's dream.* Ever since, I have loved every day and every minute of seminary, knowing it is a gift I've been given. Now that I'm nearing my doctoral graduation, my prayer is that I can nurture that gift and give it back, and this book is part of that. This is for you, Dad.

Notes

Introduction: The Story of Jesus Was

1. Susy Flory (@susyflory), "Jesus was nonviolent," Facebook, January 10, 2021, https://www.facebook.com/share/p/1EsQvF4SQc/.

Chapter 2: Jesus Was Nonviolent

1. David deSilva, *The Letter to the Galatians* (Eerdmans, 2018), 117–18.
2. J. Nelson Kraybill, *Apocalypse and Allegiance: Worship, Politics, and Devotion in the Book of Revelation* (Brazos, 2010), 57–60.
3. Nijay Gupta, *15 New Testament Words of Life* (Zondervan Academic, 2022), 58–59.
4. John Dear, "Offer No Violent Resistance (The Sermon on the Mount, Part 3)," *National Catholic Reporter*, July 10, 2007, https://www.ncronline.org/blogs/road-peace/offer-no-violent-resistance-sermon-mount-part-3.
5. Michael J. Gorman, *Cruciformity: Paul's Narrative Spirituality of the Cross* (Eerdmans, 2021), 92–93.
6. Scot McKnight, *Sermon on the Mount*, The Story of God Bible Commentary 21 (Zondervan, 2016), 126.
7. N. T. Wright, *Paul and the Faithfulness of God*, Christian Origins and the Question of God 4 (Fortress, 2013), 1492.

8. Dietrich Bonhoeffer, *Discipleship*, trans. Barbara Green and Reinhard Krauss (Fortress, 2003), 133.

Chapter 3: Jesus Was New

1. Scot McKnight, *The King Jesus Gospel* (Zondervan, 2016), 109.
2. Makoto Fujimura, *Art and Faith: A Theology of Making* (Yale University Press, 2020), 47.

Chapter 4: Jesus Was the God-Human

1. Catharina Regina von Greiffenberg, *Meditations on the Incarnation, Passion, and Death of Jesus Christ*, ed. and trans. Lynne Tatlock (University of Chicago Press, 2009), 167.
2. Gordon D. Fee, *Jesus the Lord According to Paul the Apostle: A Concise Introduction* (Baker Academic, 2018), 172–73.
3. John Goldingay, *Do We Need the New Testament? Letting the Old Testament Speak for Itself* (IVP Academic, 2015), 22.
4. Henry Scowcroft Bettenson and Chris Maunder, eds., *The Documents of the Christian Church*, 4th ed. (Oxford University Press, 2011), 27–28.
5. Von Greiffenberg, *Meditations*, 167.
6. Thomas H. McCall, *Forsaken: The Trinity and the Cross, and Why It Matters* (IVP Academic, 2012), 9, 108–9.
7. Mary Douglas, "God and Humanity Brought Together: The Incarnation as Gospel," *Evangelical Review of Theology* 45, no. 1 (2021): 63–65.
8. McCall, *Forsaken*, 44.
9. McCall, *Forsaken*, 42.
10. McCall, *Forsaken*, 46, 69.
11. Cherith Fee Nordling et al., "Which False Teachings Are Evangelical Christians Most Tempted to Believe In? Hidden Heresies Come in Many Shapes and Sizes," *Christianity Today* 59, no. 3 (2015): 26–27.

Chapter 5: Jesus Was Dependent

1. Hilary of Poitiers, "On the Trinity," in *Nicene and Post-Nicene Fathers: Second Series, Volume IX—Hilary of Poitiers*, John of Damascus, ed. Philip Schaff and Rev. Henry Wallace (Cosimo Classics, 2007).
2. Marianne Meye Thompson, *John: A Commentary*, New Testament Library (Westminster John Knox, 2015), 65.

Chapter 6: Jesus Was a Student

1. Scot McKnight, *The Real Mary: Why Protestant Christians Can Embrace the Mother of Jesus* (Paraclete, 2016), 103.
2. Scot McKnight, *The Blue Parakeet: Rethinking How You Read the Bible*, 2nd ed. (Zondervan, 2018), 230.
3. Richard Bauckham, *Gospel Women: Studies of the Named Women in the Gospels* (Eerdmans, 2002), 110.

Chapter 7: Jesus Was Not White

1. Erika Doss, "Making a 'Virile, Manly Christ': The Cultural Origins and Meanings of Warner Sallman's Religious Imagery," in *Icons of American Protestantism: The Art of Warner Sallman*, ed. David Morgan (Yale University Press, 1996), 62–65.
2. Doss, "Making a 'Virile, Manly Christ,'" 65.
3. Doss, "Making a 'Virle, Manly Christ,'" 67.
4. See Andrew Torre, "The World Is Not White," *Rutland Herald*, June 3, 2017, https://www.rutlandherald.com/opinion/commentary/the-world-is-not-white/article_61fd63e1-d401-5af7-9642-e9b52557c7ed.html.
5. Denise Eileen McCoskey, *Race: Antiquity and Its Legacy* (Bloomsbury Academic, 2019), 2–11.
6. David R. Roediger, *How Race Survived US History: From Settlement and Slavery to the Eclipse of Post-Racialism* (Verso, 2019), xii.

7. E. V. Hill, *A Savior Worth Having* (Moody Publishers, 2002), 33–34.

Chapter 8: Jesus Was a Barrier Breaker

1. See Ephesians 4:1–3; Romans 12:8; 16:17; Colossians 3:12–13; Galatians 3:26–29.
2. Dallas Willard, *The Divine Conspiracy* (HarperOne, 2009), 255.

Chapter 9: Jesus Was a Winemaker, Part One

1. Pope Pius XII, quoted in *The Quotable Wine Lover*, ed. Kate Fiduccia (Main Street, 2000), 148.
2. Andrew Curry, "Oldest Evidence of Winemaking Discovered at 8,000-Year-Old Village," *National Geographic*, November 13, 2017, https://www.nationalgeographic.com/history/article/oldest-winemaking-grapes-georgia-archaeology.
3. See Genesis 27:28; 49:11; Numbers 18:12; Deuteronomy 7:13; Psalm 104:14–15; Proverbs 3:10; 31:6; Ecclesiastes 9:17; 10:19; Isaiah 25:6–9; 61:1–11; Jeremiah 31:12; Hosea 14:7; Joel 2:22, 24; Amos 9:13–15; Revelation 19:9.
4. See the translation in *The Ante-Nicene Fathers*, ed. Alexander Roberts and James Donaldson, vol. 5 (Hendrickson, 1994).
5. Clifton Fadiman, *Any Number Can Play* (World Publishing, 1957), 203, quoted in Kate Fiduccia, ed., *The Quotable Wine Lover* (Main Street, 2000), 17.
6. See Genesis 24:31; Exodus 22:21; Leviticus 19:33–34; Numbers 35; Deuteronomy 16:11, 14; Luke 10:1–16; 14:12–14; 24:13–35; Acts 9:43–10:48; Romans 12:13; Hebrews 13:2; 1 Peter 4:9; Revelation 3:20.
7. Gisela H. Kreglinger, *The Spirituality of Wine* (Eerdmans, 2016), 12. See also 30–32, 331.

Chapter 10: Jesus Was a Winemaker, Part Two

1. See 3 Baruch 3:6–4:17; Babylonian Talmud Sanhedrin 70a.
2. Gisela H. Kreglinger, *The Soul of Wine: Savoring the Goodness of God* (InterVarsity, 2019), 77.
3. Kreglinger, *Soul of Wine*, 228.
4. Kreglinger, *Soul of Wine*, 236.

Chapter 11: Jesus Was Recentering the Commandments

1. Thom S. Rainer and Eric Geiger, *Simple Church: Returning to God's Process for Making Disciples* (B&H, 2011), 16–17.
2. Douglas R. A. Hare, *Mark*, Westminster Bible Companion (Westminster John Knox, 1996), 158.
3. Scot McKnight, *The Jesus Creed: Loving God, Loving Others,* 10th anniversary ed. (Paraclete, 2014), 9.
4. See Exodus 22:22; Deuteronomy 10:18; 24:17; Jeremiah 22:3.
5. McKnight, *Jesus Creed*, 13.

Chapter 12: Jesus Was Not Politically Powerful

1. See Isaiah 11:4–5; 42:13; 63:1–6; Luke 1:69–74; 24:21; John 6:14–15; Acts 1:6.

Chapter 14: Jesus Was Humble

1. Eve-Marie Becker, *Paul on Humility*, trans. Wayne Coppins (Baylor University Press, 2020), 3.
2. Catherine J. Wright, *Spiritual Practices of Jesus: Learning Simplicity, Humility, and Prayer with Luke's Earliest Readers* (IVP Academic, 2020), 88.
3. Becker, *Paul on Humility*, 18.
4. Scot McKnight, *Sermon on the Mount*, The Story of God Bible Commentary 21 (Zondervan, 2016), 43.

Chapter 15: Jesus Was Merciful

1. Todd Walatka, "The Principle of Mercy," *Theological Studies* 77, no. 1 (2016): 116.
2. Study note for Mark 5:25–26 in *The CEB Study Bible*, ed. Joel B. Green (Common English Bible, 2013).
3. J. I. Packer, *Knowing God* (InterVarsity, 1973), 125.

Chapter 17: Jesus Was Emotional

1. Peter Scazzero, *Emotionally Healthy Spirituality* (Zondervan, 2017), 19.
2. Stephen Voorwinde, *Jesus' Emotions in the Gospels* (T&T Clark, 2011).
3. Gerald F. Hawthorne, *The Presence and the Power: The Significance of the Holy Spirit in the Life and Ministry of Jesus* (Wipf & Stock, 2003), 29–30.
4. Lisa Feldman Barrett, *How Emotions Are Made* (Mariner, 2017).
5. F. Scott Spencer, *Passions of the Christ: The Emotional Life of Jesus in the Gospels* (Baker Academic, 2021), 3.
6. Voorwinde, *Jesus' Emotions*, 163.
7. Voorwinde, *Jesus' Emotions*, 217.
8. K. J. Ramsey (@kjramseywrites), "If you are feeling crushed by pain or fear, go to the Garden. Bear witness to Jesus's tears. Notice how his fear spilled from his body as blood . . . The God of the Garden, cross, and grave is the God who knows your name and is with you in your pain. There is solidarity in the Son," Twitter (now X), June 28, 2021, https://x.com/kjramseywrites/status/1409664983302955010.

Chapter 18: Jesus Was Subversive

1. J. Nelson Kraybill, *Apocalypse and Allegiance: Worship, Politics, and Devotion in the Book of Revelation* (Brazos, 2010), 20.

2. N. T. Wright, *Surprised by Hope: Rethinking Heaven, the Resurrection, and the Mission of the Church* (HarperOne, 2008), 50, 74, 129–31.
3. Diane Langberg, *Redeeming Power: Understanding Authority and Abuse in the Church* (Brazos, 2020), xi.

Chapter 19: Jesus Was Compassionate

1. B. B. Warfield, *The Person and Work of Christ* (Presbyterian and Reformed Publishing, 1950), 100–101.
2. Charles H. Talbert, *Matthew*, Paideia (Baker Academic, 2010), 130.
3. Walter Bauer, *A Greek-English Lexicon of the New Testament and Other Early Christian Literature*, ed. Frederick William Danker, 3rd ed. (University of Chicago Press, 2000), under "splanchnizomai."
4. R. T. France, *The Gospel of Matthew*, New International Commentary on the New Testament (Eerdmans, 2007), 373.
5. Curtis Mitch and Edward Sri, *The Gospel of Matthew*, Catholic Commentary on Sacred Scripture (Baker Academic, 2010), 139.
6. See 1 Kings 22:17; 2 Chronicles 18:16; Isaiah 56:11; Jeremiah 3:15; 10:21; 12:10; 23:1–4; Zechariah 10:2–3; 11:16.
7. France, *Gospel of Matthew*, 373.
8. See chapter 17, "Jesus Was Emotional," in this volume.
9. Walter Rauschenbusch, *Christianity and the Social Crisis in the 21st Century* (HarperOne, 2008), 16.
10. Dietrich Bonhoeffer, *Letters and Papers from Prison*, trans. Isabel Best et al. (Fortress, 2010), 45.
11. Henri J. M. Nouwen et al., *Compassion: A Reflection on the Christian Life*, rev. ed. (Image, 2006), 3–4.
12. Adapted from Augustine, *The City of God: Selections and Introduction by Hans Urs von Balthasar*, trans. William Babcock and Rachel Coleman (Ignatius Press, 2021), 9.5.
13. Nouwen et al., *Compassion*, 15.

Chapter 20: Jesus Was a Friend to Sinners and Outcasts

1. Gordon Hodson, "Why 'Love the Sinner, Hate the Sin' Doesn't Work," *Psychology Today*, April 28, 2020, https://www.psychologytoday.com/au/blog/without-prejudice/202004/why-love-the-sinner-hate-the-sin-doesnt-work.
2. Craig L. Blomberg, *Contagious Holiness: Jesus' Meals with Sinners* (IVP Academic, 2005).
3. Blomberg, *Contagious Holiness*, 128.
4. Mark A. Powell, "Jesus and the Pathetic Wicked: Re-Visiting Sanders's View of Jesus' Friendship with Sinners," *Journal for the Study of the Historical Jesus* 13, nos. 2–3 (2015): 202.
5. Scot McKnight, *The Blue Parakeet: Rethinking How You Read the Bible*, 2nd ed. (Zondervan, 2018), 167.
6. Powell, "Jesus and the Pathetic Wicked," 188–208.
7. Pete Greig, *Dirty Glory: Go Where Your Best Prayers Take You* (Hodder & Stoughton, 2016), 284.
8. Blomberg, *Contagious Holiness*, 180.

Chapter 21: Jesus Was for Women

1. Frederica Mathewes-Green, "I Met Christ," Beliefnet, https://www.beliefnet.com/faiths/christianity/2004/03/i-met-christ.aspx.

Chapter 22: Jesus Was for the Oppressed

1. See our website mksafetynet.org.
2. Robert Downen et al., "Abuse of Faith: 20 Years, 700 Victims: Southern Baptist Sexual Abuse Spreads as Leaders Resist Reforms," *Houston Chronicle*, February 10, 2019, https://www.houstonchronicle.com/news/investigations/article/Southern-Baptist-sexual-abuse-spreads-as-leaders-13588038.php.
3. Judy Carter, "About Bill Cosby: Why Did the Women Wait So Long?" *Psychology Today*, December 9, 2014, https://www

.psychologytoday.com/us/blog/stress-is-laughing-matter/201412/about-bill-cosby-why-did-the-women-wait-so-long.

4. *Collins English Dictionary*, "oppression," accessed March 24, 2025, https://www.collinsdictionary.com/dictionary/english/oppression.
5. Luke Timothy Johnson, *Prophetic Jesus, Prophetic Church: The Challenge of Luke-Acts to Contemporary Christians* (Eerdmans, 2011), 135.
6. See Deuteronomy 27:19; Psalm 82:3–4; Jeremiah 22:3; Zechariah 7:10.
7. Justo L. González, *Acts: The Gospel of the Spirit* (Orbis Books, 2001), 25.

Chapter 23: Jesus Was Loving to His Enemies

1. N. T. Wright, *After You Believe: Why Christian Character Matters* (HarperCollins, 2012), 183.

Chapter 25: Jesus Was Nonpolitical

1. Scot McKnight, *The King Jesus Gospel: The Original Good News Revisited* (Zondervan, 2011), 61.

Chapter 26: Jesus Was Forgiving

1. Lewis Smedes, *The Art of Forgiving: When You Need to Forgive and Don't Know How* (Ballantine Books, 1997), 5.
2. "Read Rachael Denhollander's Full Victim Impact Statement About Larry Nassar," CNN, updated January 30, 2018, https://www.cnn.com/2018/01/24/us/rachael-denhollander-full-statement/index.html.
3. David Von Drehle, "How Do You Forgive a Murder?" *Time*, November 23, 2015, https://time.com/time-magazine-charleston-shooting-cover-story.
4. Desmond Tutu, *No Future Without Forgiveness* (Image, 2000).

Chapter 27: Jesus Was Prayerful

1. Darrell L. Bock, *Luke*, NIV Application Commentary Series (Zondervan, 1996), 569.
2. Bock, *Luke*, 569.
3. William Barclay, *The Gospel of Luke*, rev. ed. (Westminster, 1975), 272.

Chapter 28: Jesus Was Abandoned by Many

1. Ben Witherington, *The Gospel of Mark: A Socio-Rhetorical Commentary* (Eerdmans, 2001), 399.

Chapter 29: Jesus Was Veil Tearing

1. James Strong, *The Strongest Strong's Exhaustive Concordance of the Bible*, ed. John R. Kohlenberger III and James A. Swanson (Zondervan, 2001), "G4977."
2. David E. Garland, *Mark*, NIV Application Commentary (Zondervan, 1996), 595.
3. Benjamin J. Snyder, "Mikvah," in *The Lexham Bible Dictionary*, ed. John D. Barry (Lexham, 2016), Logos.
4. Bryan C. Babcock, "Clean and Unclean," in Barry, *Lexham Bible Dictionary*.
5. Michelle J. Morris and Douglas Mangum, "Cleanness and Uncleanness, Regulations For," in Barry, *Lexham Bible Dictionary*.
6. Snyder, "Mikvah."
7. Benjamin Espinoza, "Baptism," in Barry, *Lexham Bible Dictionary*.
8. Morna Dorothy Hooker, *The Gospel According to St. Mark* (Hendrickson, 1993), 39–40.
9. Hooker, *Gospel According to St. Mark*, 44.
10. Garland, *Mark*, 44.
11. Hooker, *Gospel According to St. Mark*, 46.
12. Garland, *Mark*, 48.
13. Hooker, *Gospel According to St. Mark*, 33–34.

14. John H. Walton, *The Lost World of Genesis One: Ancient Cosmology and the Origins Debate* (IVP Academic, 2009), 67.
15. G. K. Beale, *The Temple and the Church's Mission: A Biblical Theology of the Dwelling Place of God* (InterVarsity, 2004), 66–69.
16. John H. Walton, *The Lost World of Adam and Eve: Genesis 2–3 and the Human Origins Debate* (IVP Academic, 2015), 165.
17. Beale, *Temple and the Church's Mission*, 32–33.
18. Walton, *Lost World of Genesis One*, 81.
19. Beale, *Temple and the Church's Mission*, 189.
20. Garland, *Mark*, 603.

Chapter 30: Jesus Was Instrumental in Our Adoption

1. Nancy Newton Verrier, *The Primal Wound: Understanding the Adopted Child* (Gateway, 1993), 16.
2. Lynn H. Cohick, *Women in the World of the Earliest Christians: Illuminating Ancient Ways of Life* (Baker Academic, 2009), 38.
3. *The Oxford Classical Dictionary*, ed. Simon Hornblower et al. (Oxford University Press, 2012), under "Adoption."
4. Cohick, *Women in the World*, 35.
5. Cohick, *Women in the World*, 104.
6. Nijay K. Gupta, *The Lord's Prayer* (Smyth & Helwys, 2018), 39–40.
7. Gupta, *Lord's Prayer*, 40.
8. N. T. Wright, *Paul for Everyone: Galatians and Thessalonians* (Westminster John Knox, 2004), 46–47.

Chapter 31: Jesus Was the Word

1. Brad Jersak, *A More Christlike Word: Reading Scripture the Emmaus Way* (Whitaker House, 2021), 29.
2. Christian Smith, *The Bible Made Impossible: Why Biblicism Is Not a Truly Evangelical Reading of Scripture* (Brazos, 2011), viii.
3. Smith, *Bible Made Impossible*, 4–5.

Conclusion: Jesus Is

1. Michael F. Bird, *Evangelical Theology: A Biblical and Systematic Introduction* (Zondervan, 2020), 409.
2. Scot McKnight, *The Real Mary: Why Protestant Christians Can Embrace the Mother of Jesus* (Paraclete, 2016), 107.
3. This was the conclusion Albert Schweitzer arrived at in his book *The Quest of the Historical Jesus* (1906) regarding attempts to find the Jesus of history.

About the Contributors

Tyler Callahan is an author, songwriter, and marketing director based in Indianapolis, Indiana. He holds a master's in New Testament from Northern Seminary. He, his wife, and their two kids belong to an incredible faith community in the Butler-Tarkington neighborhood of Indy, where they share their passion for embracing the tensions of faith and rediscovering God in the midst of doubt, despair, and disillusionment. You can follow him on Instagram (for music) and Medium (for theological reflections) @tylerevancallahan.

Amanda Clark and her husband Justin have served in ministry together in Vineyard churches since 2007. She currently pastors a Vineyard church in northeast Indiana. She is passionate about helping women step into their callings through teaching good theology about women in ministry. Amanda holds a master of arts in New Testament studies through Northern Seminary. Her favorite place to be is around a table with family and friends, where good food and meaningful conversation abound.

Elizabeth Daigle is a pastor and teacher at a large urban church in Pittsburgh, Pennsylvania. She has an MA in communications and creative writing from Wheaton College and is pursuing a certificate in New Testament studies from Northern Seminary. She loves to teach from the Scriptures by making them relatable and relevant. Elizabeth and her husband Tim have four adult children, five grandchildren, and a black Lab named Lucy. You'll often find her hiking and biking in the hills of western Pennsylvania.

Leo Diaz serves as a bi-vocational associate pastor and elder at Watermark Church in Tampa, Florida. He has a bachelor's in computer science and is a graduate of Northern Seminary, where he completed a master's in New Testament studies under Dr. Nijay K. Gupta. He and his wife have a son, twin daughters, and the most Christlike mini schnauzer you will ever meet. In his spare time, Leo enjoys reading, nature walks with his family, armchair quarterbacking his Tampa Bay Buccaneers, and playing chess. His writings and theological musings can be found at his Medium publication (Imago Dei Cafe) or his blog at watermarktampa.com.

Sue M. Diaz was a research librarian for thirty years and is now serving as a spiritual director at a retreat ministry in the St. Louis area. Her calling is to invite people to experience companionship with God through both Scripture and contemplative prayer. She and her husband reside in Edwardsville, Illinois. Their daughter is an artist and mechanical engineer.

Susy Flory is the *New York Times* best-selling author or coauthor of eighteen books. She is the founder of West Coast Christian Writers, a nonprofit dedicated to educating and supporting writers. She holds a master's in New Testament studies from Northern Seminary and is finishing up her doctoral studies at Houston Theological Seminary under Dr. Lynn H. Cohick. Two areas of scholarly interest for her are women writers and communicators in the ancient world, and the very early women missionaries and church planters of Ireland. She lives in the mountains of Northern California.

Terri Fullerton is a graduate of Northern Seminary (master of arts in New Testament studies) and is in the doctor of ministry program for the art of sacred writing at Western Theological Seminary. She is passionate about the words we use and stories that care for and carry us. She has been a guest writer on *Jesus Creed* (Scot McKnight's blog on Patheos), Lisa Sharon Harper's *Freedom Road* Substack, and *Red Letter Christians*. Her interests include reading, writing, traveling, hiking, snowshoeing, and photography. She welcomes you to join the conversation at Instagram, Blue Sky, Threads, and Substack, where she posts under @terrigfullerton.

Adrienne Gibson currently lives in sunny Arizona with her husband Matthew and three children. She is a licensed professional counselor who holds a master of arts in counseling from Denver Seminary and a master of arts in New Testament studies from Northern Seminary. Adrienne works with children and families who have experienced trauma, are working through the beauty of adoption, or are in need of co-parenting skills and strategies. Recently Adrienne has also been working with women in emotionally or physically abusive marriages. Her current passion is figuring out how to combine two of her areas of interest: counseling individuals recovering from past trauma, and the healing and restorative power that can be found in the church. For more on Adrienne, see valorcounselingaz.com/adrienne-gibson-lpc-1.

Peter Green is a veterinarian from Melbourne, Australia, with degrees in psychology and theology, including a master of arts in New Testament from Northern Seminary. He is an elder and on the teaching team at CityLife Church, a large multisite church in Melbourne. He is married with three adult children, one grandson, and a spoiled Maltese terrier.

Bethany Hammer serves at Propel Women, an organization dedicated to empowering and equipping women leaders to fulfill their God-given potential. Before joining Propel Women, Bethany spent fifteen years as a children's and family pastor at her church. She holds a master of arts in New Testament studies from Northern Seminary. Bethany resides in the Chicagoland area with her husband and three children.

Heather Hart writes for people who love Jesus but might find the Bible confusing at times. When she's not writing, Heather often has a camera in hand, scouting for the best bokeh. She's married with two kids and a dog and currently lives near Charlotte, North Carolina. Heather has a bachelor's in psychology and political science from Taylor University and a master's in New Testament studies from Northern Seminary. You can find her at heatherhartwrites.com.

Scott Johanningsmeier is a bi-vocational pastor at Elizabeth Baptist Church in southern Indiana. He has a degree in music technology from Indiana University and a master's in New Testament studies from Northern Seminary. Outside of ministry, Scott works in the technology installation industry. He is married to Jennifer and they have two daughters.

Sarah Bucy Klingler serves as the project manager for MK Safety Net, a nonprofit advocating for missionary kids who were abused on the mission field. She is also passionate about walking alongside those abused in the church, particularly women who experience deep wounds due to patriarchal views. Sarah is a graduate of Northern Seminary, where she completed a master of arts in New Testament studies. She and her husband Brandon live in northeast Ohio with their three teens. She enjoys being part of the preaching team at her church and writing theology for the everyday person. Find out more at sarahbucy.com.

Sheva Stephens Knott is a native of Cincinnati, Ohio, and a proud mother, daughter, granddaughter, grandmother, and life partner to a tribe of "heartbeats" who offer centering direction and motivation for greatness. She is an ordained pastor serving on the staff of the City of Promise Church in Fairfield, Ohio. She is a graduate of Syracuse University Whitman School of Business with a master of arts in professional accounting, and a graduate of Northern Seminary with a master of arts in New Testament. Sheva is passionate about writing and sharing Jesus with all who cross her path.

Cody Matchett is a pastor, teacher, and writer from Calgary, Alberta. He is the coauthor of *Revelation for the Rest of Us*, the cohost of *Kingdom Roots* podcast with Dr. Scot McKnight, and a doctoral student at Ridley College exploring portrayals of character in the Greco-Roman world. Cody is passionate about biblical literacy and engagement, psychology and philosophy, and all things coffee. He lives in Calgary with his wife Brianna, a counseling therapist; his daughter Aletheia Theodora; and his son Atticus Ignatius.

Becky Castle Miller is a doctoral student at Wheaton College, working on a dissertation about emotions in the gospel of Luke. She earned her master's in New Testament from Northern Seminary with a master's thesis on Jesus's emotions. Before moving to Wheaton, Becky, her husband, and their five kids lived in the Netherlands for eight years, serving at an international church. She is an emotion coach, writer, and speaker. Connect with her at beckycastlemiller.com.

Anne Mackie Morelli lives on the west coast of Canada. She is an educator, mentor, writer, and former Olympian. Anne is currently enrolled in a master of Christian studies program. She and her partner have been married for forty-eight years and have three adult sons and five grandsons. Her book, *When Grief Descends*, was published in June 2020. For more on Anne, see annemackiemorelli.com.

Melissa Pillman serves as a pastor and elder at Missio Dei Wrigleyville, which is one of four Missio Dei congregations in Chicago. She is a graduate of Northern Seminary, where she completed her master's in New Testament studies. She and her husband Andy have raised their three (now-grown) kids in the city but also love to retreat to their little cabin in the woods of Indiana.

Amanda Weber holds a master of arts in New Testament from Northern Seminary and a certificate in spiritual transformation from the Transforming Center in Wheaton, Illinois. She has been privileged to be part of the planting team of multiple churches and has enjoyed serving through prayer ministry, teaching Sunday school, leading small groups and Bible studies, singing on worship teams, and being a missionary in Ndola, Zambia. She lives with her husband, three children, and vivacious cockapoo in West Chicago.